GLOUCES
RAMBLES

Fifteen Country Walks
around Gloucestershire

Nigel Vile

With Historical Notes

COUNTRYSIDE BOOKS
NEWBURY, BERKSHIRE

First Published 1990
© Nigel Vile 1990

All rights reserved. No reproduction
permitted without the prior permission
of the publishers:

COUNTRYSIDE BOOKS
3 Catherine Road
Newbury, Berkshire

ISBN 0 85306 070 4

Cover photograph taken from Birdlip Hill
by Andy Williams

Produced through MRM Associates, Reading
Typeset by Acorn Bookwork, Salisbury
Printed in England by J. W. Arrowsmith Ltd., Bristol

Other counties in this series include:

Avon	Middlesex
Bedfordshire	Oxfordshire
Buckinghamshire	Somerset
Cambridgeshire	Suffolk
Dorset	Surrey
Essex	East Sussex
Hertfordshire	West Sussex
Kent	Wiltshire

Other Walking Guides available from
Countryside Books include:

Exploring the Pilgrims' Way
Exploring the Ridgeway
Walks Around the Downs
New Forest Walks
Short Walks in the New Forest
The Test Way
The Wayfarers Walk
New Forest Companion
In the Steps of Jane Austen
In the Steps of Thomas Hardy

Contents

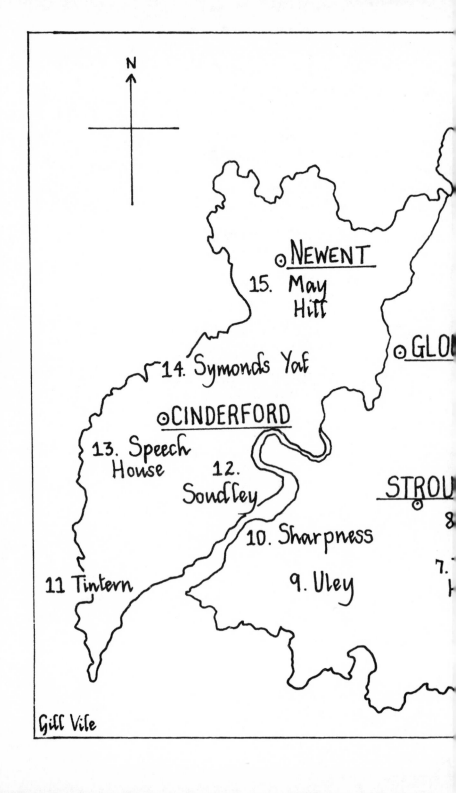

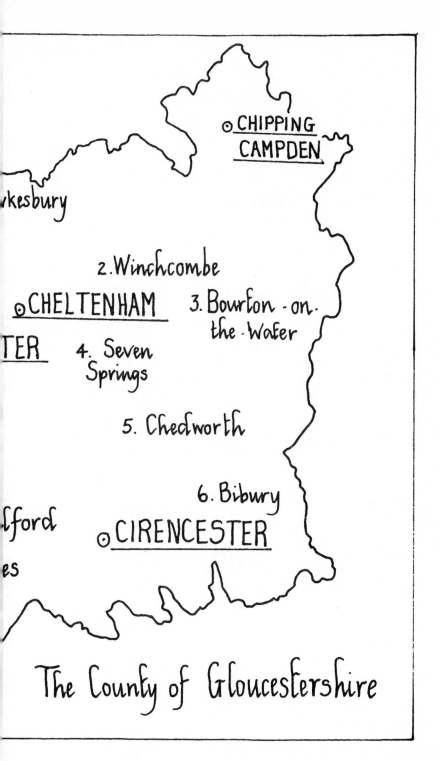

⊙ CHIPPING
__CAMPDEN__

kesbury

2. Winchcombe

⊙ __CHELTENHAM__   3. Bourton - on -
                          the - Water

TER   4. Seven
              Springs

        5. Chedworth

                6. Bibury

ford   ⊙ __CIRENCESTER__

es

The County of Gloucestershire

Introduction

Mellow Cotswold villages, the Forest of Dean with its ancient traditions and the valley of the mighty river Severn are the ingredients which give Gloucestershire its very special flavour.

The eastern side of the county is dominated by the Cotswold Hills, that land of sparkling rivers and golden cottages that has launched a thousand picture postcards and calendars. A region of high wolds, traditionally dominated by sheep and wool, now increasingly populated by the commuter with money to spare, not to mention the occasional royal! Nevertheless, the Cotswolds still manage to retain their quiet beauty and charm for the visitor prepared to seek out the silent byways and footpaths that criss-cross the region. West Gloucestershire provides a complete contrast. Dominated by the Forest of Dean, this was the land of miners and foresters, fiercely independent characters sandwiched between the Severn and the Wye who were never certain whether their allegiance lay with the English or the Welsh. The divide between these two regions is provided by one of our great rivers, the Severn. The Severn Vale is a land of grazing meadows and pastures, too susceptible to flooding to offer much scope for arable farming. Historically, the river was also Gloucestershire's arterial link with the rest of Britain, and along the estuary lie dotted any number of old inland ports from Lydney and Bullo Pill to Newnham and Sharpness.

This is a county that provides unlimited scope for the rambler, which obviously posed a considerable problem for the author! Selecting just 15 rambles from such a rich and diverse county was no small task. Hopefully, the selection of 'Gloucestershire Rambles' will provide a 'taster' of just what the county can offer the walker. The aim certainly is not to provide the 15 definitive walks in the county, rather it is hoped that the interested visitor can find in these pages an introduction to the whole spectrum of landscapes that Gloucestershire has to offer.

Each of the 15 circular rambles comes complete with details of parking and refreshment arrangements, together with approximate estimates of the distance to be covered. The timing for a ramble will, of course, depend upon the nature of the individual or group concerned. Two miles in an hour is a leisurely pace, 3½

miles an hour and the old brow would be perspiring quite quickly!
A personal selection of historical notes has also been included to
enable the landscapes and landmarks, the villages and the people
to be placed into some sort of historical context.

Each ramble was planned using the Ordnance Survey 1:25,000
series of maps, that show clearly the public rights-of-way. For
those who like to use 1:50,000 sheets, the numbers to look out for
are 150, 162 and 163. The grid reference given with each walk
relates to that walk's starting point.

I was born in that part of the county that has now been annexed
by the County of Avon. It certainly gave me a great deal of
pleasure exploring the county of my birth, and I can but hope that
some of this enjoyment and pleasure will be conveyed to the
reader of this volume.

Nigel A Vile
March 1990

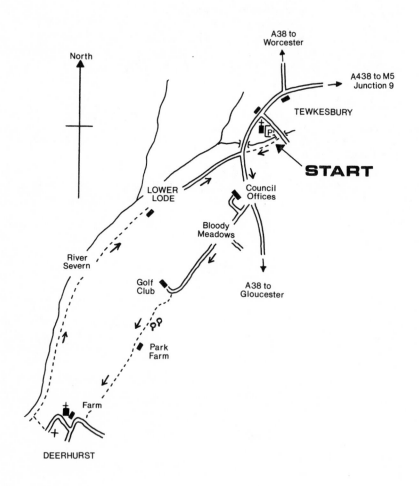

North

A38 to
Worcester

A438 to M5
Junction 9

TEWKESBURY

P

START

LOWER
LODE

Council
Offices

Bloody
Meadows

River
Severn

Golf
Club

A38 to
Gloucester

Park
Farm

Farm

DEERHURST

Tewkesbury
and the Severn

Introduction: Just where the A38 is thinking of turning its back on Gloucestershire and heading northwards into Worcestershire, lies the medieval town of Tewkesbury, filled with fine timber-framed houses backing onto the Severn. This is indeed an area with a real sense of history. Not only does Tewkesbury offer a fine abbey, built by the Benedictine monks in 1100 and spared the ravages of the Dissolution, it is also the site of a fierce battle during the Wars of the Roses in 1471. The 'Bloody Meadows' bordering the Severn received their unfortunate name when the river allegedly ran red with the blood of countless Lancastrians. Across the fields south of Tewkesbury lies the village of Deerhurst, an altogether more peaceful settlement on the banks of the Severn. The village is a veritable feast of ecclesiastical delights, possessing both a priory church and a magnificent Saxon chapel – Odda's Chapel – that can be dated precisely back to 12th April 1056. The ramble follows the banks of the Severn back to Tewkesbury along a section of the recently created Severn Way. Although no longer tidal above Gloucester, the river is still navigable and of considerable dimensions.

Distance: A generally level 5 mile circuit alongside the river Severn, taking a leisurely 2 to 2½ hours. Following heavy rain, the area is subject to considerable flooding!

Refreshments: Although there are no public houses or cafes on the walk itself, the town of Tewkesbury has an abundance of such amenities.

How to get there: Approaching Tewkesbury from the south along the A38, turn right just past the abbey into Gander Lane. The

11

turning is signposted as leading to the Recreation Ground. There is a car park at the rear of the abbey, just off Gander Lane. (GR 892325)

The Walk: Continue along Gander Lane, away from the A38, cross a stream and bear immediately to the right into the recreation ground. Follow the right-of-way that borders this stream across the 'rec' until the path passes through a handgate to join the busy A38 road. From the recreation ground, you will enjoy a fine view of the abbey unimpeded by any more recent building developments. The fine abbey church of St Mary the Virgin sits just above the meadows that border the stream.

Turn to the left and follow the A38 for a few hundred yards until you reach Lincoln Green Lane on the right-hand side. This is the access road not just to the Council Offices, but also to Tewkesbury Park, now home to a Golf and Country Club. Follow this road almost the whole way to the Club House, passing the Bloody Meadows on the right-hand side before crossing the golf course. The driveway to the Club House climbs a slight rise before veering to the right into the members' car park. Just where the road bears right, the public footpath continues across the greens to the left. Marker posts, liberally coloured with lashings of yellow paint, mark the route across the fairways to an exit stile out of the course. The route towards Deerhurst now lies across open agricultural land.

In the first field, follow the left-hand hedgerow to a stile in the next corner. In the field beyond, aim for a gateway around to the right of the copse ahead. It is best to follow the field's perimeter, rather than heading diagonally across the field itself. Once through the gateway, the path continues straight ahead, passing to the right of the farmhouse that now comes into view. About 100 yards beyond Park Farm, cross the stile on the left-hand side in the hedgerow, bear immediately to the right and continue to the top of the field. Pass through a gap in the hedgerow ahead, and a fine open view opens up across towards Deerhurst. The priory church, your next target, is especially prominent.

Follow the perimeter of the next field to a stile, almost in the bottom left-hand corner. Climb over this stile and cross to the gateway in the far left-hand corner. Just past the gateway, cross the stile on the left and pass through a couple of small fields to the nearby lane. Turn right into Deerhurst, the road bears to the left at the entrance to Priory Farm, and then take the first turning on the right signposted to Odda's Chapel and the Church. The priory church is 200 yards down this lane on the right-hand side, and a little further on you will pass the entrance to Odda's Chapel on the left. Both the church and the chapel are absolutely delightful and not to be missed.

A gateway opposite Odda's Chapel leads to a field-path that leads in a matter of yards to the banks of the Severn. Follow the river northwards (to the right!) for 1½ miles, across the occasionally flooded and muddy pastures, until you pass in front of a boathouse and join a quiet lane. Follow the lane for ½ mile until it joins the A38. Directly opposite the junction lies the recreation ground and the car park where the walk began. The town of Tewkesbury is well worth exploring before you leave.

Historical Notes

Tewkesbury lies at the confluence of a couple of navigable rivers, the Severn and the Warwickshire Avon. This is an obvious clue to the town's medieval prosperity, where river trade generated a great deal of commerce in the locality. The student of medieval architecture will find delights at every turn, for this is a town full of medieval alleys and timber-framed buildings. Perhaps the finest such example lies opposite the abbey – the Abbey Cottages. What appears to be a humble rank of 15th century cottages was in fact a bustling medieval market place. Each day, the window shutters were let down to form shop counters and business would commence. One point of interest – Tewkesbury was the inspiration for Dinah Maria Craik's *John Halifax Gentleman*. Many of the settings in the book, which tells the story of the social betterment of a poor orphan through his own efforts, can be traced in and around the town. The 19th century mill, situated quite logically in Mill Street opposite the abbey, is one of these settings. A visit to the town's John Moore Museum will shed rather more light on *John Halifax Gentleman* for here there is a collection of memorabilia associated with the book.

Tewkesbury abbey is, of course, the town's crowning glory. Technically, St Mary the Virgin is but a meagre parish church, having been purchased by the Corporation from Henry VIII at the time of the Dissolution of the Monasteries. It was built to the designs of Robert Fitzhamon in the early 12th century from Caen stone. The external layout is essentially cruciform, much restored over the years, but topped out with a most magnificent Norman tower. At 46 ft square and 148 ft in height, this is in all probability the largest such tower in existence. The inside of the abbey is well worth a visit.

The Battle of Tewkesbury: The meadows bordering the Severn were the site of a noted battle in 1471 during the Wars of the Roses. The Lancastrians had suffered a recent defeat at Barnet, a battle that both Margaret of Anjou and her son – Prince Edward – had managed to avoid due to delays occasioned by bad weather in the Channel. On their arrival in England, Margaret and the Prince set off towards Wales, where the Lancastrians were busy recruiting supporters. Crossing the Severn proved to be a problem, however. The Yorkist townsfolk of Gloucester gave them a rough reception, and the followers of the house of Lancaster were soon fleeing northwards to attempt a crossing at Tewkesbury. They had reckoned without the tactical brilliance of Edward IV, who was hot on their heels, and the Lancastrians were routed alongside the Severn. The river was said to have run red with the amount of blood that was shed, giving rise to the 'Bloody Meadows' on the edge of the town. Prince Edward was killed, Margaret of Anjou was imprisoned for 5 years before being allowed to return to France where she died in poverty. The Bloody Meadows lie on the right-hand side just before the walk enters the Golf and Country Club. There is an information board and map giving full details of the conflict.

The River Severn rises on the eastern slopes of Plynlimmon, deep in Central Wales, from where its 210 mile journey to the Bristol Channel commences. Before the railway age, the Severn was the main artery of trade in Gloucestershire and was navigable at flood time as far north as Welshpool. Local craft known as Severn trows were a common sight plying up and down the river from Iron-bridge to the estuary. Trows were shallow draught sailing vessels with a load capacity of up to 80 tons. Today, vessels carrying up to 450 tons can navigate the river to Worcester, while those carrying

150 tons can continue on to the present upper limit of commercial navigation at Stourport. At this fascinating inland port, the river is joined by the Staffordshire and Worcestershire Canal, which provides a gateway through to the vast network of waterways that enmesh the West Midlands.

Deerhurst means quite literally 'the forest of wild animals' – a description that seems wholly inappropriate when applied to the landscape in this part of Gloucestershire today. In Saxon times, this was the site of the chief monastery of Hwicce, a Kingdom of the Lower Severn. Indeed, a priory had existed here as early as the 7th century. Deerhurst was also the scene of a treaty drawn up between Canute and Edmund Ironside, redividing England between the Saxons and the Danes in 1016. The influence of the priory declined as the abbeys at Tewkesbury and Gloucester came to the fore, and the whole estate was sold to the Throckmorton family at the Dissolution. The church was converted for parish use making it quite possibly the oldest parish church in the country. The original church with its ancient nave forms the heart of the current building, although there have been subsequent rebuildings that have greatly enlarged St Mary's. These developments have been mapped out in the excellent guide book written by Dr Edward Gilbert. The church contains an early 9th century font, one of the finest in existence, richly carved with the Celtic trumpet spiral. The memorial brass to Sir John Cassy and his wife is one of just two in the country to show a named pet dog – Tirri – whilst the unique arrangement of pews in the choir around the altar, date back to an earlier Puritan style of worship.

Odda's Chapel lay hidden beneath plaster as a mere part of Abbot's Court until 1885. The nave was actually a farmhouse kitchen! The Rev G Butterworth rediscovered this delightful Saxon chapel in that year, and it has now been restored to something approaching its original glory. The Odda Stone dates the building precisely to 17th April 1056, Earl Odda – a friend of Edward the Confessor – erecting the chapel in memory of his brother.

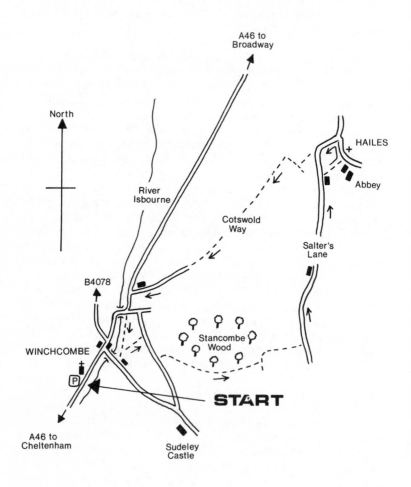

A46 to
Broadway

North

River
Isbourne

Cotswold
Way

HAILES

Abbey

Salter's
Lane

B4078

WINCHCOMBE

P

Stancombe
Wood

START

A46 to
Cheltenham

Sudeley
Castle

Winchcombe
and Hailes Abbey

Introduction: The highest parts of the Cotswold Hills lie in the north, between Cheltenham and Broadway. Cleeve Hill can boast a height of 1,083 ft, whilst Broadway Hill – at 1,024 ft – runs Cleeve a close second. The river Isbourne carves a path through this quite dramatic landscape, having its source on the slopes of Cleeve Hill, from where it flows northwards to join the Warwickshire Avon at Evesham. Sitting proudly at the head of the valley is the small town of Winchcombe. History is thick on the ground in these parts, in what was once a Saxon walled city, later to become the site of an important benedictine abbey. After a reasonably strenuous climb onto the nearby Salter's Hill, the ramble drops down to another site of great antiquity – the ruins of the Cistercian abbey at Hailes. Throughout, the views are far-ranging, with landmarks such as the Vale of Evesham and the Malvern Hills reminding us that this is border country. Five miles north of Winchcombe, just beyond the delightfully named village of Wormington, lies the boundary with Herefordshire and Worcestershire.

Distance: A circuit of 5½ miles that includes a climb of well over 500 ft onto Salter's Hill. Allowing time to explore the abbey at Hailes this ramble will make a pleasant half-day's outing.

Refreshments: There are several public houses in Winchcombe, including the White Hart Inn that lies at the end of the walk. There are no refreshment facilities on the route itself.

Directions: Winchcombe lies 6 miles north of Cheltenham, on the A46 road to Broadway. Roadside parking is available alongside the parish church, which lies on the left-hand side as you enter the town. (GR 023283)

The Walk: From the parish church in Winchcombe, continue along the A46 towards the town centre. In a few hundred yards, turn right into Castle Street, alongside the White Hart Inn. Cross the river Isbourne and, within a matter of yards, turn left along a narrow alley between Tan Yard Bank and Sudeley Mill Cottage. At the end of this alley, pass through a kissing gate and cross the field diagonally to the right. There is a right-of-way that continues directly ahead, too, but that forms the final leg of the return journey from Hailes. The right-hand side of the field dips down to a lane which you join after passing through another kissing gate.

Turn right, and in 100 yards a public footpath is signposted into a field on the left-hand side. The route lies uphill, across the fields that now lie ahead, passing to the right of Stancombe Wood. The right-of-way is so clearly waymarked that detailed directions are unnecessary. In the first field, aim for the stile diagonally to the right, beyond which you bear half left to reach a gateway at the far side of the next field. In the third field, it is half right to a gateway in the hedgerow opposite. From here to the hilltop, literally follow the left-hand field boundaries, always keeping Stancombe Wood to your immediate left-hand side, and aiming for the steady succession of stiles with clearly marked yellow direction arrows. The climb brings rewarding views back across Winchcombe, with Cleeve Hill rising impressively in the background. Sudeley Castle is another notable landmark. Right on the hilltop, you pass a gateway into an arable field, where the wall on your right is followed onto a track and thence onto Salter's Lane. The climb up from Winchcombe has been a good 500 ft!

Turn left and follow the lane downhill towards Hailes, with fine views opening up northwards towards the Vale of Evesham. At the bottom of the hill, just past a group of cottages, turn right onto a gravelled track which leads past a few more cottages and onto an open field. Hailes Abbey is located at the far side of this field.

Cross to a stile, just to the left of the ruins, and join the cul-de-sac lane that leads to the abbey. Both the church and the ruins of the Cistercian abbey, now cared for by English Heritage, are worth an hour of your time. With Hailes lacking any refreshment facilities, the abbey grounds are a suitable spot to enjoy a packed lunch.

To return to Winchcombe, surprisingly you ignore the footpath signposted to Winchcombe! Instead, follow the lane away from the abbey, past the church and onto a road junction. Turn left, cross a tributary stream of the Isbourne, and where the lane bears sharply to the left continue straight ahead along a waymarked bridlepath. In a few hundred yards, turn right onto another path, with a pair of fine old oak trees to your right. It is not long before the right-of-way bears to the left across an arable field, white discs on marker posts indicating the direction the footpath follows. You are now actually following a section of the Cotswold Way, and the path is consequently well used and well marked.

After a kissing gate, bear half right towards the distant telegraph poles. Beyond the next kissing gate, the path rises and Winchcombe comes into view ahead. If you are walking the route on a Bank Holiday or a summer weekend, a very evocative view might appear to your right as steam engines regularly ply along the preserved section of the Gloucestershire and Warwickshire Railway, just across the fields. Drop down to a footbridge, beyond which you join Puck Pit Lane. This leads in ½ mile to the A46.

Turn left, and either follow the main road back into Winchcombe or cross the stile just to the left of Isbourne Bridge and follow the field-path alongside the river. This brings you back to that narrow alley and Castle Street. Retrace your steps to the parish church where the walk began.

Historical Notes:

Winchcombe is a town shrouded in history. At one time, it was a Saxon walled city, which later became the site of a noted Benedictine abbey. The abbey was founded in AD 788 by the Mercian King Kenulf, as a shrine to his son, the boy King Kenelm. Although historians cast doubts on the story that Kenelm was murdered by his tutor on the orders of his scheming sister, the two stone coffins in the parish church – allegedly those of Kenulf and Kenelm – help in keeping the legend alive. The George Inn was a pilgrims' inn, and above its archway lie carved the initials 'RK'. Richard Kyderminster was Abbot at Winchcombe during the reign of Henry VII. Unfortunately, the abbey was razed to the ground in the 16th century during the reign of Henry VIII, leaving no visible traces for later visitors. Another interesting page in the history of the town occurred when, for a period of 50 years, tobacco was cultivated in the locality. Parliament was not amused at this development, which hindered the growth of plantations in Bermuda and Virginia, thereby reducing customs revenue. Elizabeth I signed a proclamation against Winchcombe's tobacco growers whilst, in 1619, James I levied a tax of 3d a pound on the weed. This later went as high as 6/10! The local people were naturally displeased, and matters reached such a pitch that a troop of Life Guards was sent to the district. However:

'..... the country did rise on them, about five or six hundred threatening to kill them, horse and man, so that they were constrained to depart.'

Winchcombe town hall houses a Folk Museum detailing the town's rich history. Alongside the museum is an unusual seven-holed set of stocks, supposedly constructed to accommodate a local one-legged ne'er-do-well, presumably alongside a trio of his able-bodied cronies!

Winchcombe church, which dates back to 1460, is one of the finest of the Cotswold 'wool' churches. Local cloth merchants, perhaps aware of their servitude to mammon, made a compensatory spiritual investment in the many fine ecclesiastical buildings scattered across the county. Particular features of note are the grotesque gargoyles (including a little man with wings wearing a top hat and an ugly teddy bear), a pillar almsbox hollowed out from a tree, and an altar-cloth said to have been made by Catherine of Aragon, the first of Henry VIII's many wives. Adorning Winchcombe church is a magnificent Perpendicular tower, surmounted by a massive weathercock. The bird, originally perched upon St Mary Redcliffe church in Bristol, is crafted from copper and measures 6 ft from beak to tail, and 4½ ft in height. The tower has to support its not inconsiderable frame of some three hundredweight!

Sudeley Castle lies just outside Winchcombe and, although it lies ½ mile off the walk itself, it is clearly visible from Salter's Hill. Sudeley is so beautifully located that Edward IV arrested Ralph Boteler the owner for treason in order to acquire it for himself! Boteler's last words as he was taken away were 'Sudeley Castle, thou art the traitor, not I.' During the Civil War, it was held by George Brydges, 6th Lord Chandos, for the Royalists, and came under a not inconsiderable siege. Although Brydges later defected to Cromwell's side, the Parliamentarians nevertheless well-nigh demolished the castle to prevent its use as a Royalist stronghold in the future. Sudeley today is essentially a 19th century reconstruction, although the chapel and ruined banqueting hall survive from Medieval times. The chapel houses the tomb of Catherine Parr, the sixth wife of Henry VIII. Readers of P G Wodehouse will be fascinated to learn that 'Blandings' was modelled upon Sudeley. Sudeley Castle is open to the public daily from April to October.

Hailes Abbey dates back to 1246, and was built as the result of a vow made by Richard Earl of Cornwall just four years earlier. His life had been endangered by storms when crossing the Channel, and the abbey was erected to show his appreciation for what he saw as divine providence. Richard was the son of King John, and brother of Henry III, and he was granted the Manor of Hailes to provide land for the abbey. Twenty monks of the rather austere Cistercian order, led by Jordan, came to Hailes from Beaulieu in Hampshire. In 1270, Richard's son, Edmund, gave the abbey a phial that allegedly contained the Holy Blood of Jesus Christ. This was backed up by a 'certificate of authenticity' issued by the Patriarch of Jerusalem. The phial and its silver shrine became an object of pilgrimage, raising much needed revenue for the abbey. Stories spread of how 'God daily showeth miracles through the virtues of the Holy Relics' although blasphemers were regularly condemning the whole exercise as a fraud that used nothing other than ducks' blood! These doubts reduced the flow of pilgrims to a trickle, and the Pope was forced to offer indulgences to all pilgrims to Hailes. The numbers revived – and the much needed revenue began to flow again! The abbey was dissolved in 1539, the buildings were looted and destroyed, leaving today's skeletal shell. Analysis of the phial of blood showed it to be nothing more than honey coloured with saffron, that was renewed each year! Henry VIII had the fraud publicly burned at Paul's Cross in London in 1534. The abbey ruins are open to the public, and visitors can see the location of the sacred shrine of the 'holy blood'. The site also houses a small museum that details the history of Hailes abbey.

Hailes church, alongside the abbey ruins, was the recipient of some minor embellishments from the spoils of the nearby ruin. A number of encaustic and heraldic tiles were removed across the way! The church contains a number of fine medieval wall paintings, including one of a hunting scene that is thought to represent a warning to Sabbath breakers.

Salter's Lane is one of the many 'saltways' or 'whiteways' that criss-crossed the country in centuries past. Before the advent of freezing, salt was used for preserving freshly-killed meat. These ancient trackways ran from the country's saltings to towns and villages up and down Britain. The Saltway above Winchcombe probably came from the salt town of Droitwich in the Midlands. This salt was far purer than that produced from the salt pans on the Severn. Certainly, some of the Cotswold manors had their own salt workings at Droitwich, notably Sodbury, Chedworth, Guiting and Stanway, and pack-horses carrying this essential commodity were a common sight across the hills.

WALK THREE

Bourton-on-the-Water and the Rissingtons

Introduction: Bourton-on-the-Water is quite deservedly the tourist mecca of the Cotswolds. The centrepiece, of course, is the river Windrush, running parallel to the main street and crossed by any number of low stone footbridges. All around are the most beautiful of buildings, fashioned with great skill from the local limestone and once described as 'almost unreal ..... looking more like a film-set than real life'. Arrive early, appreciate the beauty of the village before the other visitors arrive, and then head eastwards to another world – the peaceful and little-visited hamlets of Little and Wyck Rissington. The landscape is gentle and undulating, rather than hilly, and is definitely dominated by water. Having left the Windrush behind, the ramble very quickly passes through Bourton Ponds – flooded gravel pits, now a haven for wildfowl. The return from Wyck Rissington to Bourton is by means of a section of the Oxfordshire Way, and it is not long before we are striking up an acquaintance with two other Cotswold rivers, the Eye and the Dikler, both typically cool, clear and sparkling. A very English slice of landscape with its green pastures, babbling brooks, stone cottages and ancient churches.

Distance: A very gentle 5½ mile circuit that will fill a leisurely 3 hours.

Refreshments: Bourton-on-the-Water possesses countless tea-shops, inns, cafes and restaurants. There are no refreshment facilities on the route itself.

How to get there: Bourton-on-the-Water is located just east of the A429 from Stow-on-the-Wold to Cirencester, 3 miles south of Stow. The village is clearly signposted, as are the public car-parks.

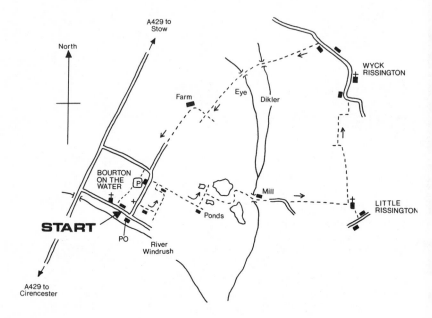

As there is a choice of parking areas, the ramble begins in the centre of Bourton, at the War Memorial alongside the Windrush. (GR 167207)

The Walk: This is such a delightful spot, that you may well be reluctant to set off on a 5 mile jaunt – but given the will-power, head south-eastwards from the War Memorial down the main street, away from the church. At the Post Office, turn left into Station Road. A little way along Station Road, follow the sign-posted footpath on the right-hand side, almost opposite the Baptist church. The path passes the backs of some houses before reaching a junction where you turn left. Follow this next path on to yet another junction, turning right onto a path alongside some allotments.

In just over ¼ mile, take the signposted path on the left-hand side, which leads into Bourton Pools. This fascinating area of flooded gravel pits houses many forms of wildfowl. Follow the

24

waymarked path through the pools, the only possible point of confusion being just beyond the first small pool on your right. Here you turn right off the main path. After passing round the southern banks of a larger pool, the path leaves this watery paradise to pass over a small bridge into an open field.

Cross the field to the gateway and stile opposite, and then cross the first footbridge across the river Eye to continue along an obvious path in front of the delightful Rissington Mill. The path crosses a stile to join the driveway to the house. Continue eastwards along this driveway and where it bears sharply to the right, follow the signposted right-of-way into the fields directly ahead. On the skyline ahead is Little Rissington church, your next target. This is reached across three fields, where a well-worn path and clearly visible stiles indicate the right-of-way.

Pass through the kissing gate into the churchyard, where a very pleasant few moments can be spent exploring St Peter's church. The graves of the men killed while serving at RAF Little Rissington lie at the eastern end of the graveyard – a particularly poignant spot. (The church lies isolated from the main village, making a detour necessary should you wish to visit Little Rissington itself).

Leave the churchyard by means of the kissing gate encountered earlier, turn sharp right and follow a field-path northwards towards Wyck Rissington. In the third field on from the church, aim for the gate in the bottom left-hand corner. The earlier fields are crossed using obvious gateways as route-markers. Once through the gateway, bear left. A signposted bridleway passes through the gateway directly ahead, but the path to follow bears right to pass through an avenue of trees that continues in a northerly direction. Shortly a track is joined which leads onto a country lane into Wyck Rissington. Continue through the village, pausing to enjoy the delightful houses and cottages as well as St Laurence's church.

Continue on past the village green and duckpond until, just beyond the last house on the left-hand side (Maces Cottage) you turn left into the fields, following a section of the waymarked 'Oxfordshire Way'. This is followed back to Bourton, with frequent markers indicating the right-of-way.

At the end of the third field on from the road, do not pass through the gateway directly ahead. Instead, pass through the gateway to the right. The right-of-way in the field beyond has been well-worn by many pairs of boots, but for the purists lies in a west-south-west direction! The obvious path continues on to Bourton, shortly crossing two rivers – the Dikler followed by the Eye.

Beyond the Eye, follow the path through the gateway in the opposite field boundary, and then on to a track crossing at right-angles. Turn right to follow the path towards Moors Farm where the track bears left to head back into Bourton-on-the-Water. The track emerges onto a road through a housing development. Continue straight on to join the main road (Station Road) and continue southwards back into the centre of Bourton.

Historical Notes

Bourton-on-the-Water: Bourton is derived from the Saxon 'burh-tun' – literally 'the farmstead near the fortification'. The fortification in question is Salmonsbury Camp (GR 175211), that has its origins way back in the Iron Age. The site was later occupied by the Romans, and it is even suggested that a temple may have existed in Bourton following the discovery of Roman drain fragments beneath the parish church. The church is mentioned in the Domesday Book as being the property of Evesham Abbey, although there have been several rebuildings since the original wooden place of worship was erected by the Saxons. The current church building is the only one in the Cotswolds to possess an 18th century classical tower, this feature being the work of a local man, William Marshall. Otherwise, the design is all Sir T G Jackson's Gothic. Traditionally, Bourton was an agricultural community, even able to boast its own cattle market. For centuries the community would have been self-sufficient with its mills and bakers, its slaughter-house and its butcher, its forge and its saddler. Today, Bourton's prosperity is based upon tourism. Visitors come to marvel at the 16th and 17th century buildings, fashioned from the beautiful Cotswold stone, that line the banks of the Windrush. As a further enticement to the tourist, there are a wide range of attractions including a motor museum, a model village, a perfumery and a bird garden.

Bourton Ponds are a series of flooded gravel pits just to the east of the village. Gravel extraction had ceased in the Windrush and Dikler valleys by the 1970s, since when the flooded pits have been carefully developed for a variety of leisure and recreational purposes. There is an abundance of wildlife. The plant species include reeds, sedges and iris, whilst dragonflies, damselflies and butterflies are especially prolific insect species. The birdlife obviously varies with the seasons, with winter being a particularly exciting time on the water as migratory species such as wigeon and pochard arrive in large numbers. Whatever the time of year, however, the keen eye could well spot a heron or a kingfisher, two resident fish-eating species.

Little Rissington church lies in splendid isolation, set apart from the present day village. The original village lay alongside St Peter's until its population was wiped out by the Black Death in 1347. Superstition and the fear of infection were the reasons for not reoccupying the original site, which was finally destroyed in the 17th century. Originally, the church belonged to the Abbey of Oseney, and ecclesiastical links date back as far as the 12th century. Today's church building is predominantly a 19th century restoration, although the chancel and much of the nave are Norman, and the tiny tower is 14th century. The eastern side of the graveyard is dominated by the tombs of 75 airmen, killed whilst serving at the RAF's Central Flying School in Little Rissington between 1938 and 1976. As many as 46 of the deaths occurred during the Second World War. The graves include those of Canadian, Australian and New Zealand pilots, together with a solitary American, and serve as a poignant reminder of the human cost of war. The RAF left Little Rissington in 1976, and presented the church with an altar cross made of plated steel at the base workshops. No longer do the skies hereabouts echo to the sound of the Red Arrows, founded at Little Rissington in 1965. The village atmosphere now is rather more peaceful, much more in keeping with the origins of the name 'Rissington' – 'Hrisen-dune' was literally 'the brushwood on the hill'.

Wyck Rissington has seen little by way of physical change for over 200 years. The village consists mainly of 17th and 18th century cottages, scattered around a delightful village green that comes complete with the almost obligatory duckpond! Naturally there is a church, which many regard as a 'Cotswold gem'. Socially, however, the whole character of the village has changed this century. For the 200 years leading up to the agricultural depression of the 1930s, Wyck Rissington was but part of the Wyck Hill Estate. The village cottages were home to estate workers – farm labourers, carpenters, gamekeepers and waggoners. The recession destroyed the estate's prosperity, the cottages were sold off, and middle-class wealth moved in. The church, like so many close to the Fosse Way, is dedicated to St Laurence. This Christian martyr, who became a deacon of Rome under Pope Sixtus II, was broiled on a grid-iron in AD 247. His crime was displaying the beggars in his charge when originally summoned to deliver the treasures of the church! The 9 ft thickness of the base of the tower suggests 12th century origins, whilst 13th century work includes the top of the tower with its unusual trefoil-pierced battlements. As a young man, Gustav Holst was the church organist, and such was his 'great promise' that the Squire provided him with a cottage over-looking the green where he could both study music and give lessons to villagers. The actual organ that Holst played is still used in the church. Within the churchyard, facing the road, is a fine yew tree. It is clipped and trimmed in the shape of a cross, a nine foot high 'living cross'.

The Oxfordshire Way runs for 65 miles from Henley-on-Thames westwards to Bourton-on-the-Water. As well as linking the Chil-terns and the Cotswolds, this footpath crosses a number of Thames tributaries, including the Thame, the Ray and the Evenlode. The Oxfordshire branch of the Council for the Preservation of Rural England was responsible for creating this path, which they de-scribe as 'running along the ancient tracks of the county, through meadows and woods, along quiet river valleys and over windy escarpments, by many a delightful village'. The Way creeps over the border into Gloucestershire to end at Bourton.

Seven Springs
and Leckhampton Hill

Introduction: A debate in Parliament was needed before the people near Seven Springs near Cheltenham would give up its claim to being the source of Old Father Thames. Although Thames Head near Cirencester is officially the source of the river, there are certainly arguments for supporting the rival claims of Seven Springs. Seven Springs is certainly the highest and furthest source from the mouth of the Thames, although in practice this is the starting point of the river Churn, a mere tributary of Isis. North of Seven Springs lies Leckhampton Hill and Charlton Kings Common, high ground on the Cotswold Edge with far-ranging views across Gloucester and Cheltenham to the distant Malvern Hills. Leckhampton Hill has been extensively quarried for its limestone, leaving in one spot the dramatic limestone outcrop known as the Devil's Chimney. This rugged rock outcrop, akin to a natural pillar, lies detached from the edge of the hillside. An exhilarating ramble, which for much of its route follows the Cotswold Way, exploring a justifiably popular corner of the Cotswold Hills.

Distance: A 5½ mile circuit, taking 2 to 3 hours, with a lengthy section along the high and exposed Cotswold Edge. Pick a clear, calm day!

Refreshments: The Seven Springs Inn is conveniently located at the end of the walk. Otherwise, pack a picnic to enjoy on Leckhampton Hill.

How to get there: Seven Springs lies a few miles south of Cheltenham, where the A435 Cirencester road crosses the A436 Gloucester to Stow-on-the-Wold road. There is ample parking

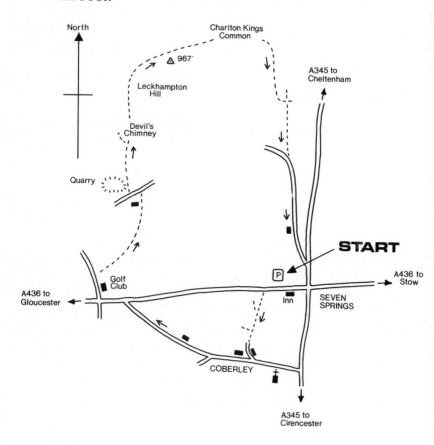

alongside the Seven Springs, which lie alongside the main Gloucester road. (GR 968169)

The Walk: Leave the lay-by alongside the Seven Springs and follow the main road in the direction of Gloucester for about 100 yards. Pass through the kissing gate on the left-hand side, and continue along an enclosed path until, at the second stile, you enter an open field. Carry straight on, keeping the hedge on your left-hand side, until you join a track that leads down to the village of Coberley. Bear left at the attractive monument on the village green, to join the main road through the village. Turn right, and pass through the pretty collection of cottages that make up this settlement at the head of the Churn Valley. The river itself lies in the dip on your left.

Ignore the left-turn on the western edge of the village, continuing straight on towards Dowman's Farm. The lane crosses a cattle-grid at this point, and the next ¼ mile is a marvellous stretch of unenclosed road walking. The Churn lies in the valley to the south, with South Hill rising beyond, some 900 ft high. Shortly, cross a second cattle-grid; the lane is once again enclosed and it is not long before you join the main A436 Gloucester road.

Turn left for a short distance along this busy road, taking due care, and then turn right at the next junction to follow the road signposted to the National Star Centre. The Cotswold Hills Golf Club lies a short distance along this road, and just past the entrance to its car park, turn right onto the bridlepath signposted to Leckhampton Hill. You have joined the Cotswold Way! Follow an enclosed track for almost ½ mile, initially alongside the golf course, until you meet a quiet country lane. Turn left, and follow the lane downhill for 200 yards until you reach the signpost on the right indicating the continuation of the Cotswold Way up onto Leckhampton Hill. The path passes the disused Salterley Grange Quarry before climbing onto the hilltop.

An obvious path follows the Cotswold Edge across Leckhampton Hill, with magnificent views westwards across Gloucester and Cheltenham towards the prominent Malvern Hills. The signposted detour to visit the Devil's Chimney should be compulsory! From this impressive rock formation, return to the Cotswold Way and continue northwards to the triangulation pillar on the north of Leckhampton Hill (967 ft). The embankments hereabouts represent the remains of the local hill fort. Almost imperceptibly, the path turns eastwards at this point to pass onto Charlton Kings Common. The views now focus upon Cheltenham, with Cleeve Hill and Cleeve Common rising impressively beyond to heights of over 1,000 ft.

There are many paths across the Common, although the route of the Cotswold Way is liberally waymarked. As a general principle, head eastwards **keeping to the level**. If the path you are following begins to plunge down the hillside, then quickly retrace your steps. Eventually, the hilltop path descends gradually to leave Charlton Kings Common and enter an open field.

Follow the perimeter of the field to reach the far left-hand corner where a path leads down to a crossroads of tracks. Turn right and follow a track onto a country lane. Continue along the lane and back into Seven Springs where the walk began.

Historical Notes

Seven Springs: Local people claim with conviction that Seven Springs is the one and only source of the river Thames. Certainly, it is farther from the river's mouth than the other contestants! In support of this claim, a plaque alongside the springs records:

> 'Hic tuus – O Tamesine pater
> Septemgeminus fons.'

In 1937, however, a Parliamentary debate failed to back the case of Seven Springs. The Minister of Agriculture was asked if he was aware that Thames Head near Cirencester was shown as the source of the Thames on the OS maps. In view of the fact that Seven Springs was a greater distance from the river's estuary, he was asked if he could make the necessary amendment on the next edition of the map. The claimants lost their appeal, however, with leading authorities all agreeing that Seven Springs was simply the source of the river Churn, a mere tributary that joined the Thames at Lechlade. This did nothing to diminish the fervour of the people near Seven Springs who are still convinced that they know best.

Coberley lies at the head of the Churn Valley, just alongside the Cheltenham to Cirencester road. At the eastern end of the village, slightly off our route but certainly worth the diversion, lies St Giles' church. St Giles has a delightful setting alongside the manor house and its neighbouring farm. The church has strong links with the Berkeley family, the wealthy landowners who owned as much as half of Gloucestershire in the 12th century. The side chapel houses the tombs of Sir Thomas Berkeley and his wife, Lady Joan Berkeley. Sir Thomas fought at the battle of Crecy in 1346, when Philip VI of France was defeated by Edward III. Lady Joan was later to remarry, her second husband was Sir William Whittington, their son a certain Richard Whittington, later to become Lord Mayor of London! Incidentally, the boundary wall south of the church, with its Renaissance openings, is all that remains of the original manor house, Richard Whittington's first home. A real rarity in St Giles' church is a 'heart burial'. In the Middle Ages, if a person of importance were to die whilst abroad, the body was often bequeathed to rest in different places. This is precisely what happened to Sir Giles de Berkeley, whose body was laid to rest in Little Malvern, whilst his heart was brought to Coberley in 1295! Although the church has ancient foundations, it was largely rebuilt between 1869 and 1872, with John Middleton as the architect.

Leckhampton Hill, rising impressively to close on 1,000 ft in height to the south of Cheltenham, is one of those places where traditionally the English have enjoyed strolling and imbibing the country air. This fact was ignored by the hill's new owner in 1902, when he erected fences and 'keep out' signs across 'his' hillside and employed a keeper to enforce his wishes. This was something that the locals simply could not stomach. En masse, hundreds of people swarmed onto Leckhampton Hill, burning down the fences and the keeper's cottage, accompanied all-the-while by a band! Traditional rights were very quickly restored. The hill's limestone has been extensively quarried over the years, and forms the building material for much of Regency Cheltenham. By 1850, the working face of the quarry on Leckhampton Hill stretched for over ½ mile. Inclined planes were soon constructed to link the quarry's tramlines with the nearby Gloucester and Cheltenham Railway, and this opened up a new market for the stone in Gloucester. In 1921, the Quarry Company built ½ mile of railway to join the GWR at Charlton Kings with the workings, and also established a number of limekilns. The venture failed, and the whole hillside was bought by Cheltenham Borough Council for free public use.

Iron Age settlers had recognised the strategic importance of the site and established a hill-fort, whose single ditch and rampart can still be seen enclosing the south and east sides of the camp. Excavations of the site in 1970 revealed pottery fragments. The hill also has poetic associations. The poet James Flecker was inspired into writing one of his last poems as he lay dying in Switzerland by the thought of:

'November evenings! Damp and still
They used to cloak Leckhampton Hill.'

The Cotswold Way runs for 95 miles from Chipping Campden southwards to Bath, following wherever possible the Cotswold Edge. As long ago as 1949, following the National Parks and Access to the Countryside Act, the idea of a Cotswold Way had been mooted by the Gloucestershire rambler Antony Drake. Plans were submitted to the National Parks Commission in 1953, acknowledged in that year's report of the Commission, but then apparently filed away and forgotten! The plan was resurrected by Gloucestershire County Council in the 1970s, and in 1975 'Operation Cotswaymark' resulted in the entire route being signposted with the now familiar arrow accompanied by a white spot. As well as Leckhampton Hill and the Devil's Chimney, the route of the Cotswold Way also passes many other landmarks including Hailes Abbey, Cleeve Hill – at 1,040 ft, the highest point on the hills, and Cooper's Hill – scene of an annual cheese-rolling ceremony. On this ramble, the whole of the route from the Cotswold Hills golf club back to Seven Springs follows the Cotswold Way.

Chedworth and the Roman Villa

Introduction: The beauty of the Cotswold Hills has as much to do with human influence as with the natural landscape. The pasture-land, the woodland and the river valleys are complemented by drystone walls, scattered farmsteads and picture-book villages, all lovingly crafted from the golden Cotswold stone. This ramble around the Chedworth area represents a perfect microcosm of the Cotswold Hills. Chedworth itself lies in a tributary valley of the Coln, its hillsides dotted with cottages linked by a network of lanes that were so obviously built before the motor age! The up and down nature of the village has been eloquently described by one writer who comments that 'it is no place for the rabid road-hog who would be distressed to find himself looking up to a doorstep and down on a chimney'. Above the village are the high wolds, undulating, open and exposed, whilst to the north lie the upper reaches of the Coln Valley, where ancient woodland has main-tained its hold to this day. On the edge of Chedworth Woods lies one of the country's finest Roman relics – Chedworth Roman Villa – now a National Trust property with public access.

Distance: A 4 mile circuit with a short section of road-walking through Chedworth village. Allow 3 hours to include a visit to the Roman villa.

Refreshments: The ramble passes the Seven Tuns Inn in Ched-worth, where bar-snacks are available.

How to get there: From Fossebridge, midway between Cirencester and Stow on the A429, follow the minor road signposted to Chedworth Roman Villa. There is parking at the villa site. Note: the villa is not at Chedworth village. (GR 053135)

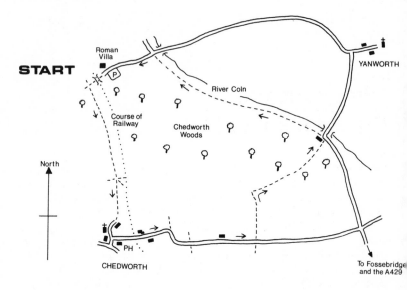

The Walk: Pass to the left of the entrance to Chedworth Villa and onto the footpath that leads into Chedworth Woods. You soon pass under an old railway bridge that carried the line from Cheltenham to Cirencester. The steps on the left lead up to the old track-bed, now a nature reserve.

Beyond the railway bridge, the path climbs gently to a cross-track. Turn left and follow the main path for almost ½ mile until it reaches a stile at the edge of the woodland. Ignore any minor paths or side turns. Cross the stile and follow the field path directly ahead, passing over (or around) a couple of old stiles, as far as a pair of handgates beneath a sycamore tree. As you cross the open fields from Chedworth Woods, there are fine views back northwards across the woodland and the Coln Valley to the high wolds beyond.

Pass through the right-hand gate, cross the small field ahead to a stone stile, and drop down a stepped path through a small patch of tree cover. Bear left along the meadow ahead. At the far end of this field, cross a stile alongside the cottage that comes into view on the right-hand side. Incidently, hidden in the dense hedgerow on your left as you cross this meadow is the trackbed encountered

36

earlier. Since the bridge near to Chedworth Villa, it has passed through a short tunnel to avoid the climb that the walker has made! With the help of a decent map, industrial archaeologists may care to seek out its two entrances. The stile alongside the cottage brings you to the edge of Chedworth village.

Continue along the road to St Andrew's church, beyond which you take the first turning on the left to pass down in front of the Seven Tuns Inn. Do not continue as far as the T-junction by the entrance to the Manor, where you would join the Cirencester to Withington road. Instead, follow the road through the village, noting where the old railway bridge has been removed. The road climbs steeply out of the village, and around a couple of bends before it emerges onto the level hilltop. There are excellent views back across Chedworth, nestling almost picture-book like in a tributary valley of the Coln.

Ignore the signposted footpaths that lead to Chedworth Villa, continuing instead along the minor road to a collection of farm buildings on the left-hand side. 500 yards beyond this point, a signpost indicates that footpaths leave the road on both sides. Turn off to the left, and pass through a gateway to head straight across the arable field ahead, back towards Chedworth Woods. A prominent sycamore tree on the far side of the field is a good landmark.

Continue down the side of the woodland beyond this tree, to a gateway on the right that leads into the woods themselves. The next ½ mile is through a delightful mixture of mature coniferous and deciduous trees, the floor a carpet of bluebells in April and May, and pheasants your constant companions. The wide woodland path emerges onto the Fossebridge to Yarnworth road. Turn left, and where this road bears right to cross the Coln, continue straight ahead along a track signposted 'Private Road – Footpath Only'. This path continues for 1 mile with the Coln on its right and Chedworth Woods to the left, eventually emerging at a minor road junction, where you turn left to return to Chedworth Villa.

Historical Notes

Chedworth Roman Villa dates from AD 120, and was quite clearly built for a rich landowner. With the decline of the Roman Empire, the villa was abandoned and lay decaying for over 1,400 years until

1864. Sometime that year, a local gamekeeper whilst digging to retrieve a lost ferret, began to unearth fragments of mosaic. The villa had been rediscovered! Its 32 rooms were laid out in three wings that surrounded a rectangular courtyard. The sophistication of the Roman culture can be gauged by the presence of hot air underfloor heating and an elaborate system of baths. There were two bath-houses that provided consecutive doses of damp heat and dry heat. This complex system of bathing was supplied with water from a spring that still runs at the site. The spring also fed the villa's Nymphaeum, a water shrine, that can still be seen by today's visitors. The bath suites and the dining room, with their fine mosaics, remain well preserved to this day. The cultured landowner was not entirely cut off from urban pleasures at Chedworth. Just 3 miles to the east lies the Fosse Way, a Roman road providing access to Corinium, better known to us as Cirencester. This was the second largest Roman town, after London, in the whole of Britain, and was founded as an administrative centre for the local Dobunni tribe. The town's excellent Corinium Museum houses a number of displays that provide a fascinating insight into the Roman way of life.

The Midland and South Western Junction Railway was formed in 1884 by the amalgamation of two railway companies – the Swindon, Marlborough and Andover with the Swindon and Cheltenham. At Chedworth, the overgrown tunnel entrances, bridges and embankments are all that remain of the course that the line followed between Cheltenham and Cirencester. The M&SW Jct shared Cheltenham Landsdown with the Midland Railway, had running powers with the GWR to Andoversford, and ran over its own metals to Cirencester. It was never a commercially successful line, its only really successful period being during the two World Wars when the route acted as a short cut for military traffic heading south. During the Second World War, the line ferried thousands of troops to the South Coast as the Western armies assembled for D-Day. The line eventually closed in 1961, and the sections of track between the Roman villa and Chedworth now form a nature reserve. The cuttings immediately above the villa contain exposures of the local oolitic limestone, where small fossil shells clearly suggest the origins of this rock type. The reserve also carries notices warning of adders, venomous snakes that can grow to two ft in length and are clearly distinguished by the zig-zag markings along their backs . . . you have been warned!

Chedworth church dates back to 1100, with the nave arcade, the tub-shaped font and the lower three stages of the tower being the chief Norman features. A hundred years later the tower was raised a further stage, whilst the chancel was rebuilt and enlarged in the characteristic Early English style of the period. In the 15th century, the Perpendicular windows in the south wall and the magnificent wine-glass pulpit were added, and the newly restored church received a visit from Elizabeth of York, wife of Henry VII. The manor adjoining St Andrew's church already belonged to her husband, and so Elizabeth also took the opportunity to visit her royal aunts. Queen Street, home of the Seven Tuns Inn, was named in commemoration of this visit. The church contains an old copy of the 'Breeches Bible'. This translation of the Scriptures was made by the English exiles in Geneva during the reign of Mary, and was the most popular Biblical translation until the Authorised Version in 1611. The 'Breeches Bible' is so-called because of the peculiar rendering of Genesis 3v17 which reads '. . . they sewed fig leaves together and made themselves breeches.'

Chedworth village is no longer home to the rural labourers and tradesmen of centuries past. Its pretty cottages are snapped up by affluent outsiders who commute to nearby towns for employment if they are not seeing out their retirement years amongst the delightful Cotswold Hills. In the 18th century, however, things were very different. An overseer of the poor drew up an inventory of a Chedworth pauper's home. Ann Coates must have led a comfortless and miserable existence with her '1 bed and 2 litle barles, one irn pot, 2 couls and a litle Cetel, one corfer and 2 boxes, one coberd and one table, one bucket, one frin pan, one binch & A pair of tongs & A Fir shul, A pear of bellis and a Pair of And Irens.' Despite the natural attractions of the locality, even William Cobbett recorded that the area presented 'a picture of dilapidation and shabbiness scarcely to be equalled'.

Chedworth Woods represent some of the oldest and most valuable woodland habitats in Gloucestershire. This is true British deciduous forest, intermingled with some conifer, where shrubs, flowering plants, ferns, fungi and lichen abound. The woods extend for some 3½ miles along the steep oolite slope on the south side of the Coln, not so much a river at this point as a large stream winding through low-lying grazing land. This tranquil woodland setting was shattered in 1833 when a Chedworth watchmaker, Giles Coates, was caught poaching by George Simpson, the local gamekeeper. Coates shot Simpson and left him badly injured, fleeing to London in a bid to escape the notorious Game Laws that then existed. He was recaptured, and subsequently tried at Gloucester Assizes. The death sentence that was imposed was later subject to a reprieve when Coates was transported to Tasmania. Somewhat ironically, the ship carrying Coates to his hard labour was wrecked en route and the luckless poacher was drowned.

Bibury and the Lower Coln Valley

Introduction: Bibury is quite deservedly one of the most popular villages in the Cotswolds. Quintessentially English, best typified by the much loved and photographed Arlington Row, this perfect rank of grey walled, grey roofed and gabled cottages front onto a millstream that trickles down to the cool, clear waters of the Coln. The Coln flows eastwards – its waters home to shoals of trout and families of mallards and coots – through a sheltered, fertile valley to the neighbouring village of Coln St Aldwyns. The riverside meadows border a pleasantly meandering waterway whose valuable fishing rights are jealously guarded. Coln St Aldwyns is another delightful village, with its much restored church and stone cottages overlooking the clear waters of the Coln and the beech woods beyond. Although lacking the drama of the Cotswold escarpment farther west, this is one of the most beautiful walks within the region. It represents a perfect introduction to the Cotswold Hills where the natural landscape and the man-made buildings blend together so perfectly.

Distance: A very straightforward 6 miles of generally level field-paths and tracks. Sections of the route are also used by horse-riders, which does mean that the going underfoot can be muddy following heavy rainfall. Allow 2½ to 3 hours.

Refreshments: There are several tea-rooms and a hotel in Bibury, and Coln St Aldwyns has a village store.

How to get there: Bibury lies 7 miles north-east of Cirencester, on the A433 to Burford. In the centre of the village, just before the road crosses the Coln, there is a parking area on the right-hand side opposite the entrance to the Bibury Trout Farm. (GR 114067)

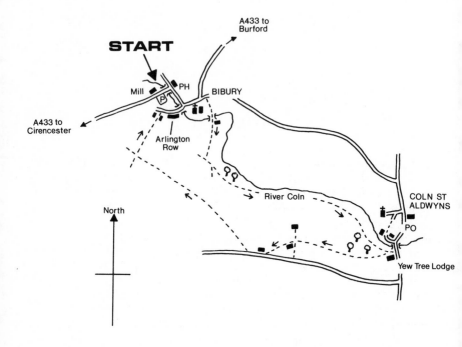

The Walk: Bibury has a magnetism that will surely make you reluctant to leave! Nevertheless, step out briskly and leave its streams and rivers, its mill and trout farm for later in the day.

Cross the Coln in front of the Swan Hotel and turn right to follow the pavement alongside the river. A quarter of a mile along this road take the right turn signposted to Coln St Aldwyns. A hundred yards along the Coln St Aldwyns road, turn right onto a signposted bridleway.

After passing in front of the magnificent Bibury Court, now an hotel, the lane crosses the Coln and winds through the buildings that make up Court Farm, before becoming an unmetalled track. Continue along the main track, avoiding any tempting right turns.

At the top of a slight rise, continue along the main track as it bears to the left. Shortly it turns to the right, but the route continues straight ahead along a grassy track. Beyond a gateway, the path follows the left-hand edge of the next field onto a handgate, where the path descends to a stile. Aim for the left-hand edge of the wood ahead, where the path passes through a gate between the trees and the river Coln.

The next ½ mile is across delightful meadowland bordering the river. This is justifiably popular walking country where thousands of pairs of feet have worn an obvious trail across the next few fields. Eventually, another patch of woodland appears ahead.

Make for the trees, keep to the edge of the wood and then clip through the far corner of the woodland onto one final open field. At the far side of this field lies Yew Tree Lodge, alongside the Coln, with the village of Coln St Aldwyns close at hand. It is certainly worth making a detour to explore the village, rather than immediately bearing right to return to Bibury from the Lodge.

The best 'circuit' of the village is found by crossing the Coln and turning immediately to the left along an access road that leads to a number of substantial houses. This road ends by a mill alongside a delightful millstream. Cross the waters by means of the footbridge, and follow the footpath on up the hill towards the church. Turn right along the road at the top of the path, having first explored the church, bear right at the village store and follow the road back to Yew Tree Lodge.

Turn right back into the field alongside the Lodge, and follow the bridleway sign to the left, up a grassy bank beneath the trees ahead. At the top of the rise, make for the gate in the left-hand corner of the field. Cross the next field, steering a course towards the house and barn ahead. A gate at the far side of the field comes out onto a track. Cross the track and carry straight on to another gateway ahead, passing to the right of a complex of farm buildings. Cross the next field, aiming for the house in the left-hand corner. Just before you reach the house, a gate on the left takes you out onto the Quenington to Cirencester road.

Turn right and, within 200 yards, right again onto a signposted footpath. This is in fact a well-defined track that will take you back to Bibury. In about 1½ miles there is a crossroads of paths, with the housing on the outskirts of Bibury visible ahead. Turn right, follow the edge of the field to an intriguing five-fingered signpost, continue straight on through a gateway and along an unmetalled road between some fine stone cottages.

At the junction ahead, turn right, drop down the hill to pass in front of Arlington Row, and you are back on the A433. All that remains is to turn left back to the Swan Inn, the Trout Farm and your vehicle.

Historical Notes

Coln St Aldwyns church has a most unusual dedication – to the 'decollation of St John the Baptist'. You can read of the poor apostle's decollation in Matthew's Gospel chapter 14, where his head was presented to Herodias in a charger! The late Norman arch in the south porch suggests that the church is at least 700 years old, although the building has subsequently suffered much at the hands of the Victorian restorers. The chancel and the two lower stages of the tower are Early English, whilst the upper stage of the tower is Perpendicular in style. Fine gargoyles adorn the exterior of the building, where there is also an interesting carving of a demon pursuing a man whose hand is firmly gripped in the Evil One's jaws! The church is cruciform in layout, with the chancel set at a slight angle to the nave to represent Christ's head inclined upon the cross. Two interesting features of an otherwise plain interior are the lancet windows at the eastern end of the church, and the font. The window glass commemorates two members of the Keble family, a father and son, both with the name John. John (Senior) was rector at Coln St Aldwyns for 40 years, whilst his more famous son (1792 – 1866) was a poet and the leader of the Tractarian Movement. Keble College at Oxford was founded in 1870 in his memory.

The font carries a Greek inscription upon its step:

'NIION ANOMH MATA MH MONANO IIN'

Translated, this reads 'Wash away my sins, wash not my face alone', but perhaps the most interesting feature of the Greek inscription is that it represents a palindrome, reading the same backwards as forwards.

Bibury, described by William Morris as 'the most beautiful village in England', owes its existence and prosperity to the river Coln. Whereas the Saxons cultivated the high wolds, their villages were always sited within river valleys where water-power existed to grind their corn. This was the original use of Arlington Mill in the centre of Bibury. The Middle Ages saw the Cotswolds develop into the centre of the English woollen industry, and a more extensive fulling mill developed on the site. It was at this time that Bibury's most photographed feature, Arlington Row, was constructed. Perhaps the most famous rank of weavers' cottages in the world, they truly represent a textbook model of Cotswold cottages. Originally built as a wool store or barn in the mid 14th century, the conversion to weavers' cottages occurred circa 1700. The marshy isle opposite Arlington Row, sandwiched between the Coln and the millstream, is known as the Rack Isle. The name owes its origins to the fact that the weavers would hang their wool on racks here to dry after it had been washed in the local streams. The 20th century saw the advent of the motor-age, giving fishermen easy access to Bibury and the Coln to fly fish for the numerous trout. In 1906, a cousin of Ruskin started the local fish farm where 40 rearing ponds stock brown and rainbow trout. Both the trout farm and the mill, now a museum of rural life, are open to the public.

Bibury church: The first ecclesiastical mention of Bibury occurred between AD 721 and AD 743 when Bishop Wilfrith of Worcester granted a piece of land by the Coln to Earl Leppa. The gift was almost certainly conditional upon a church being erected on the site. There was certainly an impressive Saxon stone church at Bibury, whilst the Domesday Book records that the local land and church was held by St Mary's Priory at Worcester. It was the Normans who lengthened the nave and added the aisles. In 1130, the church passed into the hands of the Abbey of Osney near Oxford, who held onto the property until the Dissolution of the Monasteries. It was during this period that the Early English tower was added. Of particular note internally are the Saxon jambs supporting the chancel arch, a fine 700 year old square font and the nine aumbries or wall-cupboards. Externally, the churchyard is delightful with its tidy paths lined with standard roses. The table – or bale – tombs tell of the influence of the wool trade. One part of the churchyard is known as the 'Bisley Piece' for it was here for several years that the bodies of villagers from this nearby settlement were laid to rest. Burials at their own churchyard had been forbidden in the 15th century following a brawl that had seen blood shed on the consecrated ground at Bisley. The delights of Bibury explain why the church had just 10 incumbents between 1673 and 1986, with the Reverend William Somerville performing his duties for 53 years between 1755 and 1808!

The Source of the Thames

Introduction: Its 210 miles make the Thames England's longest river, and a pilgrimage to its source must surely rank as one of life's ambitions for any true-blooded Englishman! Forget the claims of Seven Springs near Cheltenham, for the Ordnance Survey categorically declares Thames Head to be the source of Old Father Thames. The acknowledged source, at a lonely spot a few miles south-west of Cirencester, is marked by a celebratory granite slab. Do not be disappointed if you see no signs of water during a dry spell, but stand and imagine the mighty river starting its life as a tiny trickle deep underground. Despite the absence of gushing springs of fresh water the spot will surely inspire a few rousing choruses of *Rule Britannia*! High on this part of the Cotswold plateau the remains of the Thames and Severn Canal can be traced. This 18th century waterway was built to connect two of Britain's greatest rivers. At Coates, the canal pierces the Cotswold escarpment by means of a 3,817 yard-long tunnel. The classical features of its eastern portal, lovingly restored by local canal enthusiasts, represent a truly memorable piece of canal architecture.

Distance: A level 3½ miles of field-path and canal towpath, which could be easily completed in less than 2 hours.

Refreshments: The Tunnel House Inn at the eastern entrance to Sapperton Tunnel serves a range of snacks.

How to get there: Two miles south-west of Cirencester, on the A433 road to Tetbury, a minor road leads to the village of Coates. As you enter the village, park carefully on the road alongside the first group of houses that you reach. (GR 979006)

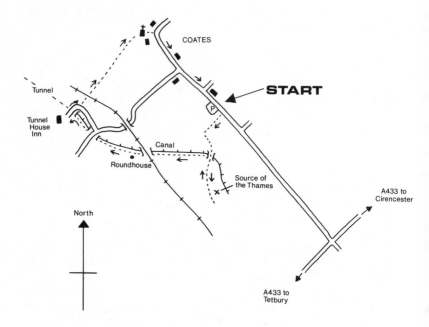

The Walk: The quest for the birthplace of Isis, as the Thames is affectionately known above Oxford, begins by back-tracking in the direction of the A433. A short distance outside the village of Coates, cross the stile on the right-hand side and follow a sign-posted fieldpath. Keep the field boundary on the right-hand side until the path reaches another stile in the corner of the field. Cross this stile and turn left to follow a well-defined track down to Trewsbury Bridge and the Thames and Severn Canal.

Cross the canal bed, pass through the gateway ahead and keep to the track as it passes through a couple of fields. Some way across the second field lies the source of Old Father Thames. The actual spot is on the left-hand side and is marked by a fine slab of granite, although water is rarely visible above ground.

Having paid suitable homage, retrace your steps to Trewsbury Bridge and descend to the canal towpath on the left-hand side. It is just over one mile along this derelict waterway to the entrance to the Sapperton Tunnel. Just after the canal passes beneath the main

London to Gloucester railway, you will discover a derelict round-house on the left-hand side which was once the home of one of the lengthmen who worked on the canal.

The canal passes through a fine wooded cutting on its final approach to Sapperton Tunnel, where the canal has been restored to something approaching its former glory. The towpath climbs the left-hand side of the tunnel entrance, to the Tunnel House Inn.

From the inn, follow the track across the top of the canal tunnel, cross the stile directly ahead and follow well-defined field paths back towards the prominent tower of St Matthew's church in Coates. Exercise extreme caution when crossing the main Gloucester railway with its '125' expresses!

The Perpendicular towered church, with its delightfully simple interior, is well worth exploring before you follow the footpath back into the village. Your vehicle will be parked a few hundred yards along the road ahead.

Historical Notes

The Source of the Thames at Thames Head is marked by a commemorative granite slab. Previously, a fine statue of Neptune had adorned the spot, but this was removed to St John's Lock below Lechlade following repeated vandalism at the isolated Thames Head site. In 1937, the Minister of Agriculture questioned the right of Thames Head to claim the title 'source of the Thames'. Seven Springs near Cheltenham was allegedly the furthest and highest source from the mouth of this great river. The member for Cirencester disputed this claim, arguing that Seven Springs was simply the source of the river Churn, a mere tributary of the Thames itself. If we accept the Ordnance Survey as gospel, then the claims of Thames Head must be upheld, for there at GR 981995 lies the legend 'Source of the River Thames'. Unfortunately, the site may be something of a disappointment with the actual source being deep underground. It is only following periods of heavy rainfall that a muddy depression will appear on the surface, and then those with vivid imaginations can perhaps picture this as the birth-place of Old Father Thames.

The Thames and Severn Canal: During the 18th century, the woollen merchants of Stroud were extremely unhappy with the high price of Forest of Dean and Shropshire coal in the town. At Framilode on the banks of the Severn, the 'black gold' was selling for just 11 shillings a ton. In Stroud, the same coal could cost as much as 22 shillings, the cross-country carriage being responsible for its doubling in price. As a result of various meetings and proposals, the Stroudwater Canal was opened from Framilode through to Stroud in 1779. Coal prices fell to just 15 shillings! It was not long before the local merchants were proposing a link eastwards from Stroud to the Thames at Lechlade, and an Act of 1783 resulted in the Thames and Severn Canal being opened just six years later. The first few miles of the canal from Stroud to Brimscombe were constructed to a width of 15½ ft, dimensions that were able to accommodate the Severn trows that worked the Stroudwater. Further east, the Thames and Severn was built to narrower dimensions which necessitated costly transhipment of through cargoes at the inland port that developed at Brimscombe. The canal was never a major success for a variety of reasons: transhipment at Brimscombe added unnecessary expense, the Upper Thames navigation was particularly poor and the canal's summit near Coates had always had problems with water supply and leaks. The subsequent story is the familiar one of railway development eating into the canal's profits, and 1911 saw the last through voyage on the waterway. Today, a Canal Trust exists and work is in progress along both the Stroudwater and Thames & Severn restoring both bed and architecture. A fitting tribute to the Trust's work is the finely restored eastern portal of the Sapperton Tunnel, passed on this ramble.

Roundhouses were built between 1790 and 1791 to house the canal's lengthmen or watchmen. These unique constructions were built of stone with stucco rendering, and the three-storey dwellings contained stables at ground level with the living-room and bed-room being housed on the upper two storeys. The roof of the roundhouse at Coates consisted of an unusual inverted cone, designed to gather rainwater. This was then piped into a storage area at ground level. Coates was near the summit of the canal, and a reliable water supply was always a problem, not only for the canal but also for the local population.

Sapperton Tunnel: 28 locks carried the Thames & Severn Canal from Stroud to its summit level, where a 3,817 yard tunnel pierced the Cotswold escarpment. Its ranking as the third longest canal tunnel in Britain is testament to the 200 – 300 men employed in its construction, at times over 200 ft beneath ground level. It is not surprising to discover that West Country and Derbyshire miners were employed on the project, many of whom were accommodated in what is now the Tunnel House Inn. Several romantic associations were struck up with local girls, and a number of the navvies were to put down roots in the area as a result! Their graves remain as a testament in Coates churchyard. The eastern portal of the tunnel is classical in style, with architecturally 'a central pediment with flanking classical columns and finials, two niches, plus two circular and a rectangular entablature'. Robert Whitworth, the canal's surveyor, confessed that the tunnel would be 'an uncertain piece of business in point of expense' due primarily to problems with the local geology. The ornate Coates' portal was in all probability a contributory factor in the tunnel's £36,578 budget being well exceeded – but then again, every canal must of necessity possess a showpiece feature!

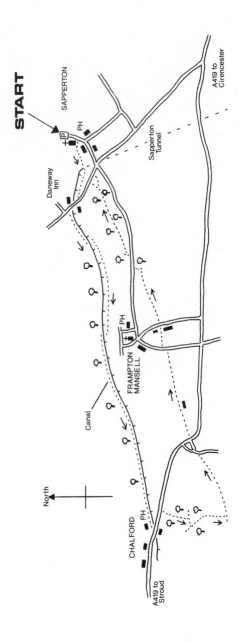

START

SAPPERTON

PH

Daneway
Inn

Sapperton
Tunnel

A419 to
Cirencester

Canal

North

PH

FRAMPTON
MANSELL

PH

CHALFORD

A419 to
Stroud

Sapperton, Chalford and the Golden Valley

Introduction: The river Frome flows from high on the Cotswolds above Sapperton, down through the Golden Valley to Stroud and on to the Severn at Framilode. East of Stroud, Golden Valley was a wholly appropriate name for an area which, during the heyday of the local cloth trade, could boast upwards of 150 mills. Golden Valley is an equally fitting description of the local landscape, for in autumn the thickly wooded hillsides turn a beautiful copper-gold colour. The valley also carried the Thames and Severn Canal from the 3,817 yard-long Sapperton Tunnel through a series of locks to Stroud, where it connected with the Stroudwater Canal and hence the river Severn. The walk follows the canal towpath from Sapperton westwards to Chalford, the centre of the local cloth trade in years gone by, returning by means of the hilltops that border the southern edge of the Golden Valley. A ramble that is packed full of interest, from the industrial archaeology of the canal and the cloth trade, through to the fine ecclesiastical architecture to be found at Sapperton church. Add the fine views from the hilltops into and across the Frome Valley, a selection of historic inns and England's second largest village whose terraces perch precariously on a steep hillside, and you have all the ingredients for a perfect day's outing.

Distance: A 7 mile circuit that initially follows the valley bottom, before climbing onto the surrounding hilltops. Whilst the valley provides shelter, the high ground can be windy and exposed. Allow 3 to 3½ hours.

Refreshments: The three villages on the walk – Sapperton, Chalford and Frampton Mansell – all have inns. Located alongside the Thames and Severn Canal is the Daneway Inn, built to house the canal's navvies and later serving as a watering-hole for the bargees.

How to get there: Sapperton lies just north of the A419 Cirencester to Stroud road, 5 miles west of Cirencester. Follow the sign to the village, and park outside of the church. (GR 947035)

The Walk: The ramble begins at St Kenelm's church in Sapperton. Bear left at the church porch and follow the path through the churchyard onto another path. Turn right, and in a few yards you will emerge into an open field. The view from this point down into the Frome Valley, with its wooded slopes, is but a taste of the many delights in store over the next 7 miles.

Turn left, follow the edge of the field for a short distance and then bear half-right towards the field boundary on the far side. There, beneath the trees, lies a stile, beyond which a footpath leads down to the western entrance to the Sapperton Tunnel. A derelict tunnel cottage lies alongside the towpath. Follow this towpath for a few hundred yards until you reach the Daneway Inn.

Cross the road opposite the inn to regain the towpath, which is followed for close on 3 miles to Chalford. Within ¼ mile, the towpath changes banks by means of a footbridge, and at the second brick bridge beyond this point, the path once again reverts to the northern side of the canal.

The Thames and Severn passes through a fine wooded valley throughout this section of its course, with the river Frome a constant companion all the while. Old woollen mills, many now converted for residential use, become increasingly common as the walk approaches Chalford, once the centre of the woollen industry in the Golden Valley. The evidence is everywhere, with the hillsides all around dotted with former weavers' cottages. The busy A419 ends the towpath part of the ramble, and while the Thames and Severn continues westwards to Stroud, we return to Sapperton across the hilltops to the south of the valley.

At the main road, turn left and follow the pavement uphill and across the London to Gloucester railway. The builders' merchants on the left-hand side occupies the site of the former Chalford Station. Shortly after the railway, turn right to follow a signposted track uphill through the woods. Turn right at the first crossroads, bear left at the next junction, and continue on uphill ignoring any left or right turns. Almost at the top of the hill, the path leaves the woodland and emerges into an open field. Follow the left-hand field boundary to the hilltop, where you turn left, keeping the wall ahead to your left. Continue across the hilltop in an easterly direction. The views below down into the Golden Valley are certainly impressive, whilst the scattered village of Chalford can be clearly seen clinging to the opposite hillside.

The fieldpath eventually passes through a gate to follow an enclosed route down to a minor road. Carry on straight across this road, following the lane opposite until you reach the busy A419. Cross the main road, and pass through the gateway opposite into the field beyond, having first crossed the access road that leads down to Westley Farm. A track is followed for almost one mile across the right-hand side of the fields ahead, passing a complex of farm buildings ¼ mile on from the A419, until you reach the Rodmarton to Frampton Mansell road.

Turn left along the road into Frampton, and in a matter of a few yards cross the stile on the right-hand side. This is just on the southern edge of the village, and a brief detour is in order should you wish to visit St Luke's church.

The main walk continues along the left-hand side of the field ahead, and on to another stile and a lane alongside a rank of houses. Cross the road and continue along the signposted footpath directly opposite. The right-of-way follows a swathe of un-ploughed turf across the fields ahead. Eventually, you will reach another stile at a corner of a wood, where you turn left to reach the Frampton Mansell to Sapperton road. The simple option is to turn right and follow the road back to Sapperton.

Alternatively, in less than 100 yards along the Sapperton road, turn left to follow a signposted path into the woodland. Shortly, bear right at a fork beneath a rather large tree and follow this footpath for ½ mile through to a large clearing. Again, fork right in the clearing and within a matter of 200 yards you will rejoin the Sapperton road, almost in the village. Continue up the road, and at the crossroads turn left into the village. Continue up the road, past the village school, until you arrive back at St Kenelm's church.

Historical Notes

Sapperton enjoys a fine location, high on the slopes of the wooded Frome Valley, with delightful views westwards in the direction of Chalford and beyond. The village sits upon the dividing line between the agricultural uplands and the industrial valleys in and around Stroud where the local wool was processed and woven in the countless mills. Although there are many handsome cottages dating from the 17th century, and quite properly built from the local stone, the highlight of the village is undoubtedly St Kenelm's church. St Kenelm's is largely a rebuilding that occurred during the early part of Queen Anne's reign, on the site of a Norman church. The Norman remains are few, the most obvious being the two side jambs to the door leading to the belfry, together with a small window alongside the belfry stairway. There are two fine monuments – one to Sir Robert Atkyns the Younger, the county historian, the other to Sir Henry Poole, whose family held the patronage of the living from the 15th century onwards.

The Daneway Inn was built in 1784 by John Nock, contractor for the Thames and Severn Canal. The building originally housed West Country and Derbyshire miners, brought into the neighbourhood to construct the nearby Sapperton Tunnel. The entrance to the tunnel lies a few hundred yards to the east of the Daneway, with its current derelict state belying its former glory. The western portal was Gothic in style and adorned with a battlemented top. To complete the picture of dereliction, alongside the tunnel entrance lie the remains of a canal cottage. The absence of a towpath through the tunnel meant that the bargees had to 'leg' their narrow-boats the 3,817 yards through to Coates and the Tunnel House Inn. The Thames and Severn had reached Sapperton and the Daneway by the summer of 1786, three years before construction work on the tunnel was finally completed. For those three years, the local community was a hive of activity, acting temporarily as the canal's terminus. Water-borne cargoes – chiefly stone, coal and timber – were off-loaded to be moved on to Cirencester and points further east by cart. Just below the Daneway is the site of the old basin, which also acted as a 'lay-up' in later years for boats waiting to use the tunnel. It was strictly one-way traffic to and from Coates, with the direction of movement being changed every 4 hours. Boats would tie up in the basin until the direction of movement was in their favour.

Chalford, one of the largest villages in England, owes its wealth and prosperity to the local woollen trade. The river Frome flowing through the valley provided the power for that many mills, it is little wonder that the local neighbourhood acquired the title of 'Golden Valley'. Chalford has been likened to an Alpine settlement due to the way that its many fine 18th and 19th century houses and cottages perch precariously upon the northern slopes of the valley. The tightly-packed rows of weavers' cottages were grouped around the mills in the bottom of the valley, whilst the merchants' houses were located on the higher slopes.

Frampton Mansell lies across the valley from Chalford. Its chief attraction is St Luke's church, built in 1843 by Lord Bathurst. Frampton Mansell, in a similar vein to Chalford, has been compared to an Alpine village. In the depths of winter, when snow is falling on the local hills, this description is not that wide of the mark. Certainly, the Italian-style church adds to the effect.

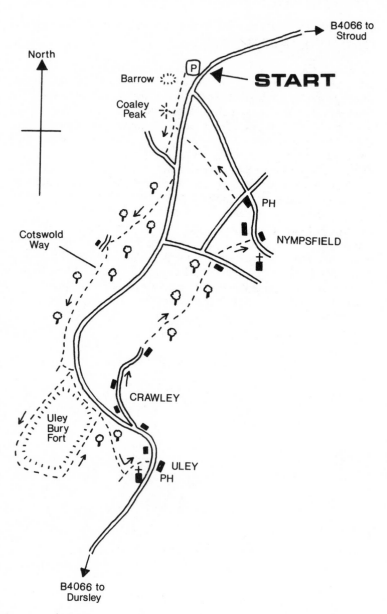

North

B4066 to
Stroud

Barrow

P

START

Coaley
Peak

PH

NYMPSFIELD

Cotswold
Way

CRAWLEY

Uley
Bury
Fort

ULEY

PH

B4066 to
Dursley

58

Frocester Hill
and Uley Bury Fort

Introduction: The most spectacular views and dramatic landscapes within the Cotswolds are to be found in and around the westward facing escarpment. The hillsides tumble quite precipitously down to the Severn vale, a drop of over 800 ft in places. The views from the hill-tops are naturally far-ranging, with landmarks such as the Severn Estuary, the Forest of Dean and the Black Mountains being but the most prominent natural features. It is little wonder that the Cotswold Way follows the length of this escarpment for 95 miles from Chipping Campden south to Bath. This ramble follows a short section of these westward facing slopes from Frocester Hill to Uley Bury hill-fort, before descending to the attractive village of Uley tucked in at the foot of the hills. Pevsner recorded no fewer than 18 buildings of note (including a beautifully built bus shelter) in what is little more than a medium sized village! Such a wealth of architecture owes its origins to Uley's former importance as a centre of the woollen trade. North of Uley, the walk continues through a cool and secluded woodland to reach the hilltop village of Nympsfield, where Pevsner recorded a mere 11 buildings of note! The return to Frocester Hill is by way of an open field-path. A fairly strenuous ramble, with one or two stiff climbs to negotiate, perhaps a small price to pay for the delightful views across the Severn to the Welsh Hills.

Distance: A relatively strenuous 5 mile ramble along hilltops that can be exposed and windswept. Watch the weather forecast before setting out! Allow 2 to 3 hours.

Refreshments: Both Frocester Hill and Uley Bury hill-fort make excellent picnic spots, whilst Uley and Nympsfield provide welcome public houses.

How to get there: The Frocester Hill Picnic Site and Viewpoint lie 5 miles south-west of Stroud on the B4066 road to Dursley. There is a large parking area at the site. (GR 795015)

The Walk: The first part of this walk follows the route of the Cotswold Way with its direction signs carrying a white dot on a yellow arrow. Frocester Hill is a fine vantage point right on the Cotswold edge, with extensive views westwards across the Severn Vale to the distant Welsh Hills. Within the confines of the site, you will find Nympsfield long barrow.

Head southwards through the gateway alongside the barrow, and continue along the fence on the right-hand side of the paddock beyond. The path follows the edge of the Cotswold escarpment, and the views are obviously quite dramatic! The silver thread of the Severn meandering across the Vale beneath is unmistakable. Beyond the gate at the far end of this paddock, bear right to the topograph. This will better answer your many questions about particular landmarks and distances.

Retrace your steps, but rather than returning to the picnic area, bear right and follow the lower waymarked path through an old quarry and up a flight of steps to the road that leads downhill from the B4066 to Coaley. Turn left to reach the main road, bear right at the top, and within 100 yards follow the signposted bridleway on the right-hand side. The path leads downhill through attractive woodland with swathes of bluebells in the spring.

Avoid any tempting side turns, simply proceed downhill for ½ mile to a lane alongside a cottage. A signpost indicates the continuation of the path, to the left, onwards and upwards through the trees. The Way crosses a couple of tracks as it climbs steadily on towards Uley Bury, passing another disused quarry face before reaching a junction of paths.

Leave the Cotswold Way, instead bearing left to emerge onto the B4066. Immediately, turn right along the signposted bridleway, bear right at the next gateway and you will have reached the northern corner of Uley Bury, the finest hill-fort in the county.

Follow the path around three sides of this Iron Age earthwork, perhaps pausing at the many vantage points to enjoy the views. Westwards lie a trio of Cotswold outliers – Cam Long Down, Peaked Down and Downham Hill. As you turn northwards to skirt the eastern edge of the fort, the views below centre on Uley, with its church being your next target.

At the end of the eastern (ie third) rampart, follow the sign-posted bridleway on the right-hand side to the woods below. Continue through the gateway ahead into the trees, pass through the woodland to another gate, and enter the open field beyond. Bear left, follow the edge of the woodland, all the while looking out for a stile at the bottom of the field to the right of the church. Cross to this stile, follow the path beyond to a junction and turn left to reach St Giles church. Outside the church, turn left to follow the road past the Old Crown Inn and on to the village green with its cluster of Georgian houses much admired by Pevsner.

Continue along the pavement beside the B4066 as it climbs out of Uley and on up Crawley Hill. In ¼ mile, just beyond Crawley House and the adjoining bus shelter, turn right along a cul-de-sac lane. Follow this lane as it passes by the collection of cottages that make up the hamlet of Crawley, and continue as far as the last residence, a relatively modern house alongside a collection of old farm buildings. The views to the right all the while are of a fine yet anonymous Cotswold valley, overlooked by the towering ramparts of Uley Bury hill-fort.

The lane ends and continues as a footpath to the left of the house, on into the woodland. Follow the path through the trees, always keeping the right-hand edge of the woodland close at hand and avoiding any tempting left turns. The tree cover lasts for about a mile until a final short sharp ascent brings you onto a lane alongside a cottage just to the south of Nympsfield. An ancient milestone indicates that this is the route of the old Gloucester to Bath coach road.

Cross the stile opposite, and in the field beyond bear to the right of the rank of houses in front. Once level with the houses, aim for the stone-slab stile in front of the old school directly ahead. A slight detour along the road to the right will bring you to St Bartholomew's church.

Otherwise turn left into the centre of Nympsfield and continue on to the Rose and Crown Inn. Turn left at the crossroads alongside the hostelry, and in a matter of 100 yards follow the signposted footpath on the right-hand side. This crosses an open field to reach the B4066. Opposite is a stile leading back to the topograph and the picnic site where the walk began.

Historical Notes

Uley Bury Hill-Fort is perhaps the finest and most complete Iron Age hill-fort within the county. Rectangular in shape, the fort sits majestically astride a hilltop promontory, with natural defences on three sides. The hillsides tumble away very steeply to the Severn Plain, some 800 ft below. If that were not enough to deter the would-be invader, then a system of terracing and embankments was added to make the natural slopes even steeper! The fort encloses an area of some 32 acres, the interior being privately owned arable land. Fortunately, a public path follows the external fortifications. Excavation of the north-eastern defences in 1976 produced evidence of Middle Iron Age occupation (circa 300BC), whilst finds from the ploughed interior would suggest that the hilltop was in fact occupied prior to the Iron Age. Aerial photography has revealed cropmarks that indicate the existence of hut circles and enclosures within the actual ramparts.

Uley enjoys a most picturesque location, almost at the head of the Cam valley east of Dursley. One interpretation of the name 'Uley' is a 'yew tree glade or clearing', and certainly there is a great deal of woodland on the surrounding hillsides. The village is like so many in the Cotswolds, owing its original prosperity and wealth to the West of England woollen trade. Business reached its peak during the Napoleonic Wars, when the Uley blue cloth was second only to the Stroud scarlet in terms of reputation. Uley's fine broad cloth gave birth to as many as 18 fulling mills in the village, and a not inconsiderable number of ale houses! Samuel Rudder, the Gloucestershire historian, likened the ale houses to 'seminaries of vice' that were the cause of much 'idleness and debauchery'.

With the decline of trade in the 19th century, and the parallel rise of the Yorkshire mills, Uley's economy hit rock bottom. The population dwindled as the able-bodied men and their families sought work elsewhere. Many migrated to the new ironworks in South Wales, others found employment as navvies on the expanding railway network, whilst some sought their fortune in Australia or Canada. The sick, the old and the infirm who were left had to fall back upon the pittance offered by the poorhouse, where the records tell us that 'crust water' was a common suppertime drink! Even the local undertaker was criticised for the workmanship on the coffins he produced for the 'Poor of Uley'. The gentleman in question, a Mr Holloway, did not seem to consider it part of his business 'to screw the tops on the coffins for his 9 shillings payment'.

The cloth trade has left a rich legacy of houses, the best of which surround the green alongside St Giles church. This is a rebuilding of 1857–58 by the architect S S Teulon. The earliest building on the site was Norman. Roger de Berkeley gave the church of Uley to the Monastery of Gloucester in the time of Gilbert the Abbot (1139–1148). Perhaps the most memorable feature of Uley church is its spectacular situation, high on a bank overlooking the valley, with the churchyard falling away abruptly to the south.

Nympsfield lies sheltered in a fold of the hills, just behind the Cotswold edge, at a height of some 800 ft above sea-level. The most obvious translation of the place-name is 'the field of Nym', although a more appropriate interpretation reads 'the open place on stony ground'. Stone is everywhere used as a building material, and such fine old buildings as Bell Court, White Hart Court and the Rose and Crown Inn stand as monuments to the Cotswold limestone. St Bartholomew's church is largely a rebuilding of 1861–63, although the 15th century Perpendicular tower, with its battlements and gargoyles, is testament to an earlier age. The rebuilding represents Teulon at his simplest, with few of his usual eccentricities save perhaps the peculiarly leaded windows. The population of the village was at its greatest during the heyday of the local woollen industry, when many broadweavers resided in Nympsfield. The area had seen far earlier waves of settlers, however. A Roman road ran through the village and down the nearby escarpment to the Severn crossing at Arlingham, whilst the nearby Frocester Hill Picnic Site houses Nympsfield long-barrow. The remains of this burial chamber lie exposed to the elements since the removal of the original mound covering. The barrow was constructed from large upright stone slabs, with the drystone entrance being a more recent rebuilding. Excavations of the 90 ft long tomb revealed 17 individuals, as well as pottery vessels and a flint leaf arrowhead.

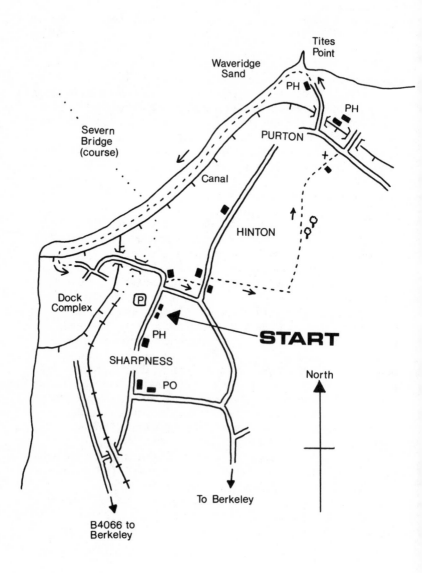

Tites Point

Waveridge Sand

PH

PH

PURTON

Severn Bridge (course)

Canal

HINTON

Dock Complex

P

START

PH

SHARPNESS

PO

North

To Berkeley

B4066 to Berkeley

Sharpness and
the Severn Estuary

Introduction: The Severn immediately below Gloucester is not a waterway to be approached lightly. With its massive tidal range, its mud and sand flats and a notorious horse-shoe bend, only the most seasoned of navigators would take a vessel this way. To facilitate access to Gloucester, a ship-canal was cut from Sharpness to the city. The Gloucester and Sharpness Canal completely by-passed the perilous upper reaches of the estuary. At Sharpness, warehouses and cranes, quays and timber-yards will fascinate the industrial archaeologist. From the bustling wharves, the ramble crosses a network of field-paths to the neighbouring village of Purton, returning by way of the canal towpath and the banks of the Severn where the mud-flats provide a feeding ground for many birds. With views of both the estuary and the Forest of Dean beyond, with the remains of the original Severn Bridge, and with a graveyard where literally dozens of barges lie rotting away, this is truly a fascinating insight into Gloucestershire's gateway to the sea.

Distance: A very straightforward 4½ miles of field-path and canal towpath, with no real gradients to negotiate, taking a leisurely 2 hours.

Refreshments: In Sharpness, a little way along the road from where the walk begins is the Pier View Hotel. Purton can offer the Berkeley Hunt Inn alongside the canal, and the Berkeley Arms Inn on the banks of the Severn Estuary.

How to get there: The B4066 links the A38, some 12 miles south of Gloucester, with Sharpness. As you enter Sharpness, turn right under the railway rather than continuing along the main road into the docks. In ¼ mile, turn left by the shops to follow the B4066 as it passes above the dock complex. A little way beyond the Pier View Hotel, park carefully alongside some bungalows on the right-hand side, a short distance before the minor road leading to Purton. (GR 677027)

The Walk: Continue along the road until, just a few yards beyond the turning for Purton, you cross a stile in the hedgerow on the right-hand side. In the field beyond, follow the left-hand hedgerow through to a gateway in the corner. Head straight across the next field to the gate opposite (not the one in the right-hand corner!) and continue straight on through an old orchard to join the lane to Purton.

Emerging onto the road alongside the interestingly named 'Malt House Cottage' turn left. The simple option is to follow the lane through the hamlet of Hinton and on to Purton, a mile or so of quiet road walking. The more intrepid explorers can follow the somewhat more complicated directions that take us across various fieldpaths to reach the same village.

A few yards down the lane in the direction of Purton, take the signposted footpath on the right-hand side, through a gateway opposite a bungalow. Follow the left-hand hedgerow to a gate at the bottom of the field, and in the next field follow the telegraph wires in the general direction of the far right-hand corner and another gateway. Away to the east rise the impressive slopes of the Cotswold escarpment. In the next field, make for the gateway in the far left-hand corner. In the large open field beyond, the next target is the hand-gate that is clearly visible to the left of the woodland directly ahead. A solitary oak tree half-way across this field acts as a guide-post.

Continue on beyond the woodland, keeping the fence initially to the right, later switching to the left as the right-of-way passes through an obvious hand-gate. The third field on from the wood-land slopes down to Purton and the Severn Estuary. A magnificent view opens up that embraces not only the estuary and the New Grounds at Slimbridge, but also the distant Cotswolds, the Gloucester and Sharpness Canal and the Forest of Dean.

Cross this field, dropping down to the gate at the bottom that lies to the left of Purton's church. The church, incidentally, is not an immediately obvious landmark, being the humble possessor of a somewhat uninspiring pinnacle rather than a lofty tower or spire! Beyond the gateway, the path passes to the right of St John the Evangelist church, before emerging onto the road. Opposite lies a swing-bridge across the canal. Turn left, continue along the road for a short distance to the next swing-bridge and cross the canal to follow the lane signposted to the Berkeley Arms Inn (not to be confused with the Berkeley Hunt Inn that fronts onto the canal at this point).

If you followed the lane down from Sharpness, rather than crossing the fieldpaths to Purton, you will have rejoined us at this swing-bridge. The Berkeley Arms Inn has a splendidly isolated location, overlooking the estuary and fronting onto the New Grounds at Slimbridge, seasonal home to thousands of migratory geese.

The path passes in front of the inn before bearing to the left to follow an enclosed course down to the river. This is a particularly atmospheric location, reminiscent of the landscape in Gallico's *Snow Goose*, with mud flats and swirling tides. The canal is up to the left, and is joined just beyond the rank of canal cottages up ahead.

Initially, the towpath passes through a BWB wharf before continuing for the mile or so back to Sharpness. Always, the canal is to the left, the estuary to the right. Other than the views, the return journey is full of interest – bird-life on the mud flats to interest the ornithologist, dozens of decaying Severn barges scattered along the banks of the estuary to sadden the heart of the boat-lover, and the remains of the original Severn Railway Bridge a few hundred yards out of Sharpness to fire the industrial archaeologist's imagination.

As the canal enters Sharpness, a cut on the left-hand side takes the waterway into the New Dock of 1874, where sea-going vessels of up to 5,000 tons can be accommodated. The towpath continues along the original canal to end in the Old Dock of 1827, complete with the original entrance lock into the Severn. The approach to the Old Dock is now a marina, full of colourful craft that have found this remote cul-de-sac of the inland waterway system.

Cross the canal by means of the lock alongside the chandlery – a short distance before the Old Dock basin – climb the steps ahead and continue along the lane above. Beyond the gate, the lane bears right at the top of a rise and then drops down into the heart of the Sharpness dock complex with its fascinating jumble of warehouses, cranes, timber stockpiles and disused railway lines.

Bear left at the road at the bottom, almost immediately turn left again to take the 'high level' road across the docks and railway track bed towards the prominent red-brick house on the hillside – formerly an inn, now the Severn Bridge Nursing Home! The road bears right in front of the Nursing Home to return you almost immediately to your vehicle.

Historical Notes

The Gloucester and Sharpness Canal was constructed in the early 19th century to by-pass the shallow meandering waters of the upper reaches of the Severn Estuary. Built as a ship canal able to accommodate vessels of up to 800 tons, the canal effectively made Gloucester a major inland port. Robert Whitworth surveyed the proposed route in 1784, construction commenced in 1794, and by 1827 the canal was completed from Gloucester to Sharpness. The original plan had been to join the Severn at Berkeley Pill, a proposal that was abandoned for reasons of economy. The grand dimensions of this 16 mile long canal, in particular its 90 ft width, make it second only to the Manchester Ship Canal in terms of importance and tonnage handled. At Purton, two swing-bridges cross the canal, and the village boasts a typical example of a bridge-keeper's house complete with stucco and painted doric columns, an architectural feature that was fashionable in the early 19th century. The ponds alongside the canal at Purton are timber ponds, formerly used for storing uncut timber afloat before it was towed upstream to the sawmills at Gloucester. Other than a multitude of pleasure craft, occasional coastal oil tankers work the waterway to Gloucester, creating an astonishing sight as they pass through the surrounding open fields of Gloucestershire.

Sharpness Docks were constructed where the Gloucester and Sharpness Canal joined the river Severn. The Old Dock, consisting of a small basin, a lock house and the original entrance lock from the Severn, was constructed in 1827. Within 40 years, the basin was so congested that a new larger dock was essential. The New Dock was opened in 1874, and is able to accommodate ocean-going vessels of up to 5,000 tons. This was essentially a green-field site for the port, and the Sharpness New Dock Company therefore had to construct a complete dock village, including shipping offices, terraced housing for the dock workers and a school for their children. Today, the docks appear to be thriving, with new warehouse development continuing apace.

The Severn Railway Bridge was completed on 17th October 1879, six years after the formation of the Severn Bridge Railway Company. The bridge linked the GWR and the Severn & Wye lines at Lydney with a branch of the Midland Railway at Sharpness. This gave the Midland easy access to the Forest of Dean and its collieries. The bridge consisted of a series of wrought-iron bow-string girders resting on cast-iron pillars filled with concrete. Its size can be imagined when it is remembered that it took 21 spans to cross the Severn, plus a swing bridge to span the Gloucester and Sharpness Canal! This, the third longest railway bridge in Britain, was ironically just an obscure outlet for Forest of Dean coal! Sadly, other than a couple of pillars either side of the canal, the bridge is no more. On a foggy night in October 1960, as the flood tide raced upsteam, an oil tanker missed the entrance to Sharpness Docks. It ran on and crashed into the railway bridge, a couple of spans collapsed, the boat burned out and five of the crew perished. Despite talk of repairing the structure, nothing materialised and demolition commenced on 24th August 1967.

The New Grounds north of Purton, hundreds of acres of mud flats bordering the Severn, are part of the Slimbridge Wildfowl Trust. The Trust was established in 1946 by the late Sir Peter Scott, on land owned by the Berkeley family. Signs opposite the Berkeley Arms Inn at Purton emphasize the importance of the New Grounds for wildfowl, public access being strictly limited. The reason is quite simple – this is the wintering ground for 5,000 white-fronted geese, over half of the British population of this Russian-breeding species. The New Grounds are also winter home for up to 400 Bewick's Swans, 5 per cent of the European population, as well as the occasional whooper swan.

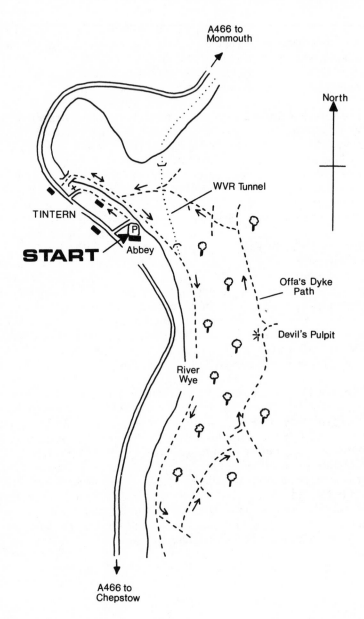

A466 to
Monmouth

North

WVR Tunnel

TINTERN

START

Abbey

Offa's Dyke
Path

Devil's Pulpit

River
Wye

A466 to
Chepstow

70

Tintern Abbey
and the Wye Valley

Introduction: South of Monmouth, the river Wye marks the Welsh border, as well as the boundary between Gloucestershire and Gwent. It is an area with a distinct border feel, with the rather more undulating landscape to the east quite suddenly rising towards the wild and rugged Welsh hills and mountains. As far back as the 8th century AD, King Offa of Mercia decided that his kingdom needed some element of protection against the various Welsh tribes, and constructed the well known dyke that bears his name. This defensive fortification runs high on the hilltops on the English side of the Wye. This particular ramble explores the Wye Valley in and around Tintern, with its celebrated Cistercian abbey. Although the ramble begins alongside this abbey in the County of Gwent, it very quickly turns to follow the eastern bank of the Wye across in Gloucestershire. From the river bank, a severe climb of 600 ft takes the rambler to Offa's Dyke path, high on the hilltops above Tintern. The rewards are views that are worth every single drop of the perspiration involved! The landscape is particularly dramatic, with woodland clambering up steep slopes that are occasionally punctuated by rugged rock formations such as the Devil's Pulpit. It is said that the devil perched himself atop this pinnacle of rock in order to hurl insults at the monks in the abbey below. A challenging walk, in an area that through the years has been an inspiration to artists, poets and writers, most notably Turner and Wordsworth.

Distance: A 5 mile circuit that involves one steep ascent and an equally steep descent. Allow 2½ to 3 hours.

Refreshments: Tintern has a variety of refreshment facilities, including two public houses. Better still, pack a picnic to enjoy high up on the Offa's Dyke path.

How to get there: Tintern lies 5 miles north of Chepstow on the A466 road to Monmouth. There is a large car-park alongside the abbey. (GR 534001)

The Walk: From the abbey car-park, follow the river bank upstream along a path signposted 'Tintern Trail', aiming for the girder bridge across the Wye, a few hundred yards ahead. The river bank path soon joins a lane; bear left here past the Methodist church and onto the A466. Turn right, continue along the pavement for a short distance, and turn right again just beyond Abbey Mill to cross the river. The bridge ahead originally carried a branch of the Wye Valley Railway into the Tintern wireworks, a branch whose course the ramble now follows through to the WVR itself.

Once across the Wye, turn right and follow the track through the trees, parallel to the river. Within a couple of hundred yards, a path forks off to the left, signposted to the Devil's Pulpit. Ignore this tempting diversion, keeping instead on the main level path alongside the river Wye. There are fine views across to Tintern Abbey at this point. Before long, the path emerges into what appears to be a clearing. This was the site of the junction where the Tintern wireworks branch joined the WVR. On the left is a tunnel entrance that took the main Wye Valley line on towards Monmouth.

The ramble continues southwards, following the old trackbed, for just over one mile to a distinct fork. Bear left, up the hill and away from the Wye, following the waymarked permissive path to the Devil's Pulpit. The route to this landmark is clearly signposted, and directions are probably superfluous . . . but just in case something has happened to all of the little yellow arrows, a few instructions might save many hours of fruitless walking in the Forestry Commission woodland!

Continue on up the hill for a short distance, and turn left at the first junction. Within 200 yards, cross a wide forest track and continue on the path uphill through the woods, ever onward and ever upward! At the next cross-track, bear left for 50 yards and then turn off the main track to follow a path on the right-hand side up a short sharp climb to reach Offa's Dyke path. My notebook recorded 'phew' at this point, over 600 ft of climbing from the banks of the Wye.

Turn left and follow Offa's Dyke path for ½ mile to the rocky pillar known as the Devil's Pulpit. On the way, you will pass a seat dedicated to: 'Chris Pugh Wye Valley Warden 1972 – 1983' handily positioned alongside a clearing in the trees that brings superb views down towards Tintern and along the Wye Valley. Certainly a spot that will detain you!

From the Devil's Pulpit, continue northwards along Offa's Dyke, in the direction of Monmouth, for about ½ mile. At this point, leave Offa's Dyke path and follow the left turn downhill signposted 'Tintern 1'. Descend to a cross track and follow the path opposite on down the hillside. This follows a mixture of natural stone steps and the man-made version. At the next junction, bear right, all the while following the yellow arrows signposted to Tintern.

Continue downhill to the river, ignoring one obvious right turn signposted to Brockweir. Rejoin the path that was followed at the outset, bearing right to reach the iron girder bridge that will return you to Tintern. Cross the bridge and turn left to reach the car-park where the walk began.

Historical Notes

The Wye Valley Railway, running from Chepstow to Monmouth, was opened with great expectations in 1876:

> 'Whilst opening up a new district hitherto unapproached by railway traffic, the new line will prove a great convenience not only to the locality through which it runs, but to the travelling public at large.'
>
> (Monmouthshire Beacon 21.10.1876)

The cost of the project came to £300,000, a sum that included stations at Tidenham, Tintern, Bigsweir and Redbrook, as well as a couple of tunnels. There were indeed great hopes as far as the financial prospects of the line were concerned. Not only would the Wye Valley Railway serve the local villages, there were also high expectations of revenue from the already well developed tourist trade. When the tin-plate works at Redbrook, the paper-mill at Whitebrook and the wireworks at Tintern were added to the formula, the expected annual revenue of some £37,000 did not

73

appear too unrealistic. Unfortunately, the line was opened just as the local industries were feeling the pinch of competition from the newly industrialised Midlands and South Wales regions. The first decade of operations saw income average out at around the £5,000 mark! The 14½ mile journey from Chepstow to Monmouth took a full 50 minutes to complete, a journey time that registers a most leisurely 17 mph. By the 1950s, the line was losing £13,000 each year, too much for British Railways to stomach even in the pre-Beeching era. Passenger services were withdrawn in 1959, with freight traffic passing the same way just five years later. Just north of Tintern, the old station has been preserved in its former pristine condition, complete with original railway signs, furniture and advertisements. The site is now a tourist information centre, where displays detailing the complete history of the WVR can be seen.

Offa's Dyke was constructed during the 8th century AD. King Offa of Mercia, a kingdom that approximated to central and southern England – which was later to include East Anglia – was the most powerful of the Anglo-Saxon monarchs. He reigned throughout Mercia from AD 757 to 796, during which period this defensive earthwork was constructed along the Welsh border from Prestatyn in the north to Chepstow, a distance of some 150 miles. As well as a defensive frontier, the dyke acted as a powerful tool of social organisation, enabling trade to be controlled and cattle raids to be curtailed. The dyke's construction is far from uniform because each landowner along its course was given the responsibility for erecting his particular section of the fortification. The most common dimensions of the frontier were a bank 6 ft in height and 60 ft wide, with a ditch on the western side. Today, the course of the dyke can be readily traced for about 80 miles, and a long-distance footpath bearing the same name follows its route wherever possible.

The Devil's Pulpit is a natural rock formation, akin to a stack, that lies alongside Offa's Dyke high above Tintern. Legend maintains that the devil sat upon this pillar of rock, preaching bawdy and raucous sermons to the monks down below in the abbey. There is no evidence to suggest that he ever succeeded in his ambition of tempting them from the virtuous life!

74

Tintern Wireworks: A wall plaque in the abbey car park, erected in 1962 by the National Brassfounders Association, commemorates the site as the birthplace of the British brass industry. While this claim is open to dispute, the site was certainly home of the first British wireworks, founded in 1566. At that time, wire making had been perfected on the Continent, but production standards in Britain were so poor that the finished product was of little use for the woollen industry, its main market. William Humphrey of the Royal Mint in London obtained a patent for its manufacture in England, and proceeded to bring skilled workers across from Saxony and Westphalia. A purpose-built works was established at Tintern. The power at the site was provided by four waterwheels, and there were also two furnaces and four hammers at the complex. The woollen industry needed wire for carding and baling. The iron used in the production of wire has to be tenacious and ductile, properties that English iron lacked. To overcome this difficulty, another German expert was brought across to Tintern to manufacture the necessary 'Osmund' iron. A foundry was established at nearby Monkswood in 1568. After changing hands several times, the wireworks closed down in 1870, although a tinplate mill continued operating on the site until 1901.

Tintern Abbey: Founded in 1131, the building the visitor sees today is a 13th century rebuilding undertaken by the austere order of Cistercian monks. Viewed against the fine setting of the Wye Valley, with thickly wooded hillsides tumbling down to the river bank, Tintern is surely one of the most beautiful of ruined abbeys. Following its dissolution in 1536, the abbey was neglected by its owner the Duke of Beaufort for many years. The roof lead had been melted down, the bells had been removed, and what was left was a magnificent collection of soaring arches framed within a 'wild secluded scene'.

The abbey ruins are open to the public throughout the year.

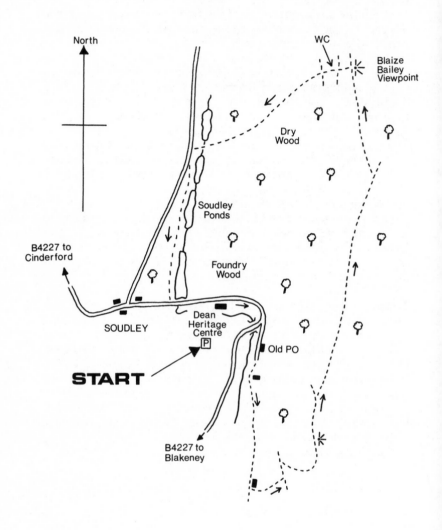

North

WC

Blaize
Bailey
Viewpoint

Dry
Wood

Soudley
Ponds

B4227 to
Cinderford

Foundry
Wood

SOUDLEY

Dean
Heritage
Centre

P

Old PO

START

B4227 to
Blakeney

The Dean Heritage Centre and Soudley Ponds

Introduction: The Forest of Dean has always been a fiercely independent region. Sandwiched between the Wye and the Severn, and with no major road or rail links with the outside world, it has owed no real allegiance to either England or Wales. Some observers have even described the Forest as being a country of its own between England and Wales! Originally a royal hunting chase, the region's economy has evolved to embrace forestry, mining and grazing, while today's forester has to face the 'realities' of the outsider in the form of the tourist! This ramble is centred upon the Dean Heritage Centre at Soudley, a former mill, that today houses a wealth of exhibits relating to the history of the Forest of Dean. From the Heritage Centre, the walk climbs to the Blaize Bailey Viewpoint, bringing fine views to the east of the Severn Estuary as it negotiates the vast horseshoe bend at Newnham. The return is by way of Soudley Ponds, man-made pools formed by damming the Soudley Brook. Originally constructed to provide water power, the Ponds today are an absolute haven for freshwater life.

Distance: A 4½ mile walk, with a height difference of 400 ft between the Heritage Centre and Blaize Bailey. The ascent is considerably more gentle than the descent! Allow 2 to 3 hours.

Refreshments: The Dean Heritage Centre houses a snack bar where light meals and soft drinks are available.

How to get there: Leave the A48 Chepstow to Gloucester road at Blakeney, to head northwards on the B4227 towards Cinderford. Within 3 miles, you will reach the Dean Heritage Centre at

Soudley. There is ample room for parking at the Centre. (GR 664106)

The Walk: Return to the B4227 from the Heritage Centre and turn right. Shortly, where the main road bears to the right to cross Soudley Brook, continue straight ahead to follow a cul-de-sac lane. This junction is marked by a phone box.

The scattered collection of cottages dotted around this delightful clearing in the Forest make up the settlement of Lower Soudley. With the sounds of running water and sheep in the background, the setting might seem idyllic, but the presence of an old mineral line in the valley serves as a reminder of the harsher realities of Forest life.

The lane passes the Old Post Office and the entrance to the disused Haie Hill railway tunnel, before it ends up as a driveway to a house. Bear right here to follow the public bridleway that skirts the right-hand edge of the hillock ahead. Continue along this wooded path, meadowland bordering Soudley Brook below to the right, for just ¼ mile. At this point, you will reach a rank of cottages on the left-hand side.

Follow the footpath on the left that borders the end wall of this rank into an open field. Cross this field to a stile in the far left-hand corner which leads into Glastonbury Wood. Carry straight on for a short way until you reach a track. Turn left, and in no more than 100 yards join what is obviously a major forest trackway. Follow this to the right as it climbs uphill, bearing to the left at the hilltop. Here, the views to the east are magnificent, embracing the Severn Vale, the estuary and the distant Cotswold Hills.

Continue northwards along the main forest track for ¼ mile until, at a distinct fork, bear right onto a quieter and more secluded pathway. Continue along this path, ignoring the occasional paths that come in on both sides, until the next fork. Bear left to follow the main track uphill to reach the Blaize Bailey Viewpoint. The fine views eastwards are again across the Severn Estuary, with the horseshoe bend at Newnham being especially prominent.

Immediately behind the viewpoint, there is a short flight of steps. Follow these onto an enclosed path that continues through the trees to an information board and WC. Cross the main track ahead, and follow the footpath signposted to Soudley Ponds. A well-worn path continues downhill through the trees to the Ponds, with white arrows painted on the trees pinpointing the actual route.

The path emerges in the valley bottom in between the first two ponds, and passes out onto the Soudley to Littledean road. Turn left, following the roadside verge, before leaving the road to follow the path that borders these delightful stretches of fresh-water back to the Heritage Centre. The path always keeps to the western banks of the Ponds, never crossing the feeder streams to reach the opposite banks. Just beyond the final pool, the path emerges onto the B4227 where a left-turn very quickly brings you to the Heritage Centre where the walk began.

Historical Notes

The Dean Heritage Centre: The tranquil rural idyll of the Forest of Dean is very quickly shattered once the inquisitive observer begins to scratch beneath the surface. From Celtic times onwards, the Forest was quarried for its iron-ore, and disused workings – or 'scowles' – can be found dotted across the local landscape. At Clearwell, just to the south of Coleford, an old iron mine has been lovingly restored to provide an exciting excursion for the visitor into the bowels of the earth. The trees of the Forest were felled in large numbers to produce charcoal, vital for the smelting process. Charcoal hearths, flattened circular pits, still litter the Forest floor as evidence of this past activity. From the 1800s onwards, the need for charcoal diminished as local coal deposits were exploited and mines sprang up throughout the region. Although the larger commercial pits have now closed, a handful of free-miners still work the seams. Men born within the hundred of St Briavels, who can claim mining ancestry, are entitled to extract the local coal. Drift mines lie in odd corners of the Forest, small-scale workings that often appear to be little more than a motley collection of garden sheds alongside a hole in the ground! The Heritage Centre, housed in a restored mill building alongside Soudley Brook, contains a collection of attractive displays that document the history of the Forest of Dean, its people, its industries and its unique way of life. The era of the coalfield is well-documented, with a colliery beam engine, a reconstruction of a miner's cottage, and occasionally charcoal burning can be seen.

The Haie Hill Railway Tunnel carried the Forest of Dean Tramroad from the mines around Cinderford to the ports of Bullo Pill and Newnham on the Severn Estuary. Bullo Pill, a tidal creek used simply for boat-building until 1800, was transformed by the Tramroad Company into a flourishing coal port. The part that Bullo Pill played in the development of the Forest's coalfield cannot be underestimated. The original 'plateway' was constructed in 1809, which makes Haie Hill one of the earliest railway tunnels in the world. The line was later operated by the GWR, having been relaid to their 'broad gauge' of 7 ft 0¼ in in 1854, and narrowed to the 'standard gauge' of 4 ft 8½ in in 1872. At its peak, the line carried 20,000 tons of coal a year down to the estuary, as well as offering a passenger service to the citizens of Cinderford between 1900 and 1958. The line was finally closed to all traffic and the track lifted in 1969.

The Blaize Bailey Viewpoint offers a magnificent panorama across the Severn Plain and the river estuary to the Cotswold Hills, some 10 to 15 miles away. The river below the viewpoint twists around a tortuous horseshoe-bend that, in the days before the Gloucester and Sharpness Canal, provided a notorious passage for craft heading up to Gloucester. It is clear from Blaize Bailey how the landscape around us is very much shaped by the underlying geology. The Severn Plain is formed from soft shales and mudstones that erode and weather easily, whilst the high ground either side of the river – the Cotswolds and the Forest of Dean – is built of hard sandstones and limestone. The stretch of river below Blaize Bailey is where the Severn Bore is given a real impetus. Just below the horseshoe-bend, a band of hard rock forms a step in the river's bed. This constriction, combined with the bottle-neck effect produced by the horseshoe itself, causes a funnelling of the incoming tide. The huge tidal wave is at its most spectacular on the spring tides, when many visitors converge on the village of Minsterworth, a few miles below Gloucester, to witness this world famous natural feature.

Soudley Ponds are a series of man-made lakes that were formed by damming the Soudley Brook. It was thought for many years that the Ponds were simply 'hammer ponds' constructed to help supply water power to drive the waterwheels at Camp Mill (now the home of the Dean Heritage Centre). Recent research, however, suggests that the Ponds date back no further than 1850 and were built for a very different purpose – to serve as fish ponds! This tradition is maintained to this day, with the first pond being a trout fishery for local fishermen. The water in the ponds is unusually clear, a property that results from the filtration process that occurs as the springwater from higher up the valley passes through the local sandstone. This unpolluted water supports a host of 'clean water organisms' with the result that the site has been declared a Site of Special Scientific Interest. An informative leaflet detailing the rich flora and fauna of the Soudley Ponds is available at the Heritage Centre.

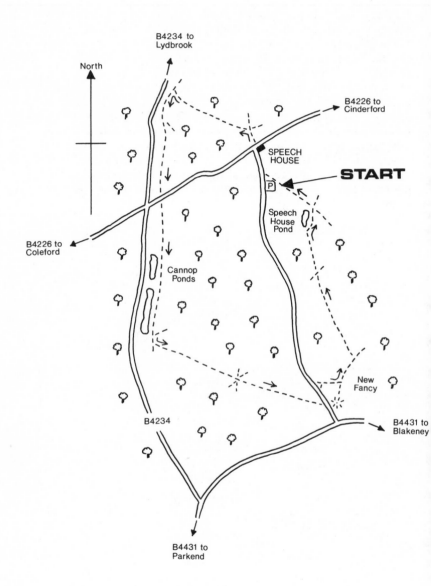

B4234 to
Lydbrook

North

B4226 to
Cinderford

SPEECH
HOUSE

START

P

Speech
House
Pond

B4226 to
Coleford

Cannop
Ponds

New
Fancy

B4234

B4431 to
Blakeney

B4431 to
Parkend

Speech House
and Cannop Ponds

Introduction: Speech House lies at the very heart of the Forest of Dean, an area of dense oak woodland and great beauty. Built during the reign of Charles II, when the Crown was reasserting its authority over the Forest, the Speech House contains the historic Courtroom of the Verderers of the Forest of Dean. In the surrounding woodland lie many other reminders of the Forest's past. The man-made Cannop Ponds acted as a reservoir of water power for the iron-works at nearby Parkend. At the southern end of the ponds lies the Forest's last surviving stone-works, where local pennant sandstone is processed. Towards the end of the ramble, we pass New Fancy, an old colliery site whose former spoil tip is now a fine viewpoint. Linking these various sites are ancient trackways and disused railroads, formerly vital lines of communication within the region. Sadly, the collieries are no more, but the undisturbed beauty of the Forest remains, an ancient Royal Forest extending to over 50 square miles.

Distance: A generally level 5 mile circuit through dense woodland in the heart of the Forest of Dean. Allow 2½ hours at a leisurely pace.

Refreshments: The facilities at the hotel would probably not be available to the rambler equipped with rucksack and boots. The best idea is to bring a packed lunch to enjoy at Cannop Ponds.

How to get there: Speech House lies midway between Cinderford and Coleford on the B4226. Turn off onto the minor road alongside the Speech House, and in 200 yards you will find the Speech House Arboretum parking and picnic area on the left-hand side. (GR 622118)

The Walk: Return to the road, turn right, in a few minutes reaching the Speech House Hotel. Opposite the hotel's main entrance is an obelisk that marks the centre of the Forest of Dean. Head into the woods beyond this monument. A stile leads into the woods by the Edward VII yews where you continue straight ahead for 100 yards to a crosstrack.

Turn left and follow the path ahead for ¾ mile until it drops down to the old Severn and Wye Railway. Ignore the many left and right turns that deviate from the main path, but do not ignore the magnificent woodland sculpture entitled *Place* that sits proudly overlooking the Cannop Valley. This is but one of the many sculptures that form the Forest of Dean Sculpture Project.

Climb up onto the old S&WR trackbed, turn left and continue for almost a mile southwards to the Speech House road, ignoring one tempting left turn en route. Cross the road and continue along the old trackbed opposite, where one or two cars may be encountered since the iron railroad has now been converted into an access road to the Cannop Ponds picnic site.

The smaller northern pond soon comes into view on the right-hand side, and it is a more pleasant alternative to leave the main track and to follow instead the waterside path. Beyond the car-park and picnic area the trackbed continues southwards towards Parkend, and the larger southern pond soon comes into view, almost ½ mile in length. Once again, a more pleasant alternative is to follow the path that borders the pond.

At the pond's southern end, follow the path signposted on the left to 'Speech House 1¾ miles'. Across the S&WR trackbed, there are two woodland paths. The left-hand path, via a stile, leads back to Speech House, but the route to take is the right-hand path that will eventually bring you to the New Fancy Viewpoint.

Over the next mile or so there are several crosstracks and side turns, but keep straight ahead all the while. The only point of confusion might be beneath some fine old oaks, at the top of a rise, where six paths meet! At this prominent crosstrack, midway between Cannop Ponds and New Fancy, cross the main track and continue along a less well-defined path almost opposite but in fact ever so slightly to the left.

The path eventually emerges at the Speech House road. Turn left and it is only a matter of yards to the New Fancy Viewpoint and picnic site. It is somewhat ironic that an old spoil-tip has now become a tourist attraction for New Fancy is in fact an old Dean colliery!

Having taken in the view from the viewpoint, follow the signs to the toilets and the start of the forest trail. Continue along the path below the toilet block to a junction, turn left and within 300 yards left again onto a path that runs parallel to the old Severn and Wye Mineral Loop Line. In just over ½ mile there is a crosstrack. Continue straight ahead along a less well defined forest-path which eventually emerges through some gorse bushes onto the southern banks of Speech House Pond.

Follow the right-hand bank of the pond to emerge onto Spruce Ride at its far end. Turn left along the ride and in less than ½ mile you will reach the Speech House Arboretum parking area where the walk began.

Historical Notes

The Speech House is one of the few buildings in the Forest of Dean that would hold out any delights for the student of architecture. Built between 1676 and 1680, during the reign of Charles II, it became the Forest's headquarters as well as housing the Verderer's Court. It was in the Court Room that disputes over the exact nature of common grazing rights and the entitlement to be a 'Free Miner' extracting the Forest's coal were settled. Constructed of local stone in the Restoration style, the Speech House is dominated by its hipped roof, dormer windows and large chimneys. It is still Crown Property, although today it is leased by an hotel chain. The Court once possessed power over life and limb. For killing the King's deer, a serf might be executed whilst a man of higher rank would escape with a fine of 5 shillings.

The Forest of Dean Sculpture Project is a collection of works of art in materials indigenous to the Forest – stone, wood and iron – located along a trail some 4 miles in length. The aim of the project is to produce sculptures that are related to certain sites in the Forest and which in some way interpret this special environment. On the ramble, we come across two of the fifteen sculptures that currently form this most unusual artistic project. Overlooking the Cannop Valley is the huge throne-like structure entitled *Place*, constructed from Forest trees by Magdalena Jetelova, a Czechoslovakian now resident in Germany. On the left-hand side, shortly before the Severn and Wye Railway, lies Tim Lees' sculpture *Rose in Hand*. This piece takes its name from the disused drift-mine above which it is located, and is a carving made out of a six-ton piece of stone hewn from a local quarry. The project has been organised by the Arnolfini Gallery in Bristol and is worthy of a special visit. A descriptive leaflet that describes the route and its various sculptures can be obtained from the Dean Heritage Centre at Soudley.

The Severn and Wye Railway Company was notable as the only tramroad in the area to become an 'edge' railway in its own right, and remain independent for upwards of 80 years. Opened in 1810, this plateway ran from the Severn at Lydney to the Wye at Lydbrook, with numerous branches. The Company adopted steam traction in 1864 and broad gauge edge rails in 1868. Standard gauge was laid in 1872. When the Severn Railway Bridge was opened in 1879, the line extended from Sharpness to Lydbrook Junction, with branches to Coleford and Cinderford. The S&W was the principal railway company in a Forest mazed with track, largely all serving the local coal trade. For example, 1¼ million tons of the 'black gold' were forwarded by rail on the S&W in 1923. Since the final closure of the line in 1970, the Dean Forest Railway Preservation Society has taken over and restored a section of track between Lydney and Parkend. The wooden station building at Norchard is actually an original S&W station from Drybrook Road Junction in the Forest. The Steam Centre at Norchard is open throughout the year, but visitors should phone Dean 43423 to find out exactly when engines are in steam.

Cannop Ponds are man-made and date from the early 19th century. The ponds were formed by damming Cannop Brook, and the resulting reservoir of water power fed the nearby Parkend iron-works. 1½ miles south of the ponds lay the works, whose 51 ft diameter waterwheel was fed by means of a lengthy stone-lined leat. At the time, this was reckoned to be the largest waterwheel in England. The head of water at Cannop was the ultimate power source that drove the bellows at the blast furnace as well as the mechanical hammers at the forges. The iron-works were demolished in 1908, leaving the ponds as a rich wetland habitat for the Forest's wildlife.

Speech House Lake was formed in 1974 as a result of damming Blackpool Brook with the purpose of forming a wildlife reserve. The gently shelved margins of the lake encourage a variety of waterside plants, creating a habitat that attracts dragonflies and other insects, as well as mallard and moorhen. The waters of the Blackpool Brook were described as being 'gouty' by the local miners on account of their orange-brown colour. In fact, this was nothing other than the local iron lending a peculiar colouration to the soil.

The New Fancy Colliery was operational between 1832 and 1944. During its lifetime, as much as 3½ million tons of coal was extracted from beneath this one spot in the Forest, extraction that also saw almost a million tons of shale and other pit waste being generated. This formed the vast spoil tip that dominates the site today. In fact, the original tip was far more impressive than the remains that today's visitor sees, for in 1961, two thirds of the spoil was removed to Llanwern in South Wales and used as the basis for the vast steel-works just outside of Newport. The remaining spoil was grassed over to create a splendid viewpoint that forms the centrepiece of a Forest picnic-area. The view from this point is perhaps the finest to be had across the Forest.

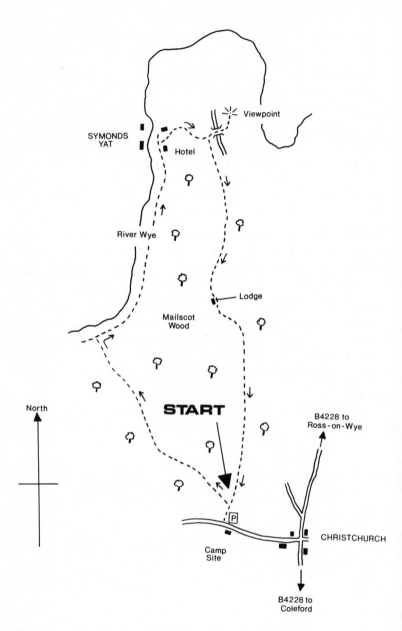

Viewpoint

SYMONDS
YAT

Hotel

River Wye

Lodge

Mailscot
Wood

North

START

B4228 to
Ross-on-Wye

P

CHRISTCHURCH

Camp
Site

B4228 to
Coleford

WALK FOURTEEN

Symonds Yat
and the River Wye

Introduction: Few rivers can match the tranquil beauty of the Wye, as it gently meanders between meadows and steep wooded slopes. This ramble combines the delightful Wye Valley, in and around Symonds Yat, with some fine woodland walking through the northern part of the Forest of Dean. It is well worth making a really early start to see the Wye Valley at its very best as the mist gently rises from the river. The highlight of the circuit is undoubtedly the famous viewpoint at Symonds Yat Rock, which provides a bird's eye view of the river as it traces out a giant loop around Huntsham Hill. From the viewpoint it is also possible to observe the nesting site of peregrine falcons. This delightful walk is full of interest throughout. The woodland and riverside paths, the scenic Wye gorge and the village of Symonds Yat itself, all combine to produce an almost perfect circuit.

Distance: A 4½ mile circuit, which does involve a rather steep ascent from the river Wye to the viewpoint at Symonds Yat. Allow 2 to 3 hours.

Refreshments: There are inns, restaurants and tea-rooms at Symonds Yat, where a traditional ferry links the two banks of the Wye. There is also a refreshment hut at the Yat Rock picnic-site, which lies on the route.

How to get there: One mile north of Coleford, on the B4228 Ross-on-Wye road, turn left at Christchurch along the cul-de-sac road signposted to the local camping site. On the right-hand side of the road, opposite the site shop and reception area, is a parking area. (GR 569129)

The Walk: From the parking area, continue along the road until, 100 yards past the camp-site reception area, you turn right into the woods along a path signposted as 'Forest Trail'. Almost immediately, turn left to follow the footpath signposted to the river Wye. For the next mile or so, follow the white arrows downhill through an area of dense mixed woodland, ignoring all of the left and right turns and forks. Eventually, you will reach a small stream whose banks are followed down to the river Wye.

Turn right and follow the path signposted to Symonds Yat East. The river will be your constant companion for the next 1½ miles as you follow the trackbed of the long-disused Ross and Monmouth Railway. Steep-sided wooded slopes line the river on both banks. At Symonds Yat East, as opposed to Symonds Yat West which lies across the river, you will find the Royal Hotel. Just past the hotel, a footpath is signposted to Yat Rock.

Follow this steep zigzag path as it climbs the hillside, often with the help of steps, to reach the Yat Rock Viewpoint carpark and picnic site. Naturally, you will make the brief detour to the viewpoint which, as well as providing fine views of Symonds Yat village clinging to the hillsides above the Wye, also enables the ornithologist to observe the nesting falcons on Coldwell Rocks.

At the southern end of the Yat Rock carpark, follow the signposted 'Forest Trail' for 1½ miles to return to the start of the ramble. The path passes through Mailscot Wood, following yellow arrows, and is well-defined throughout. There is one distinct fork, beneath a large oak tree, where you bear left. Otherwise, simply stick to the straight and narrow. The walk leaves the wood to join the road by the Christchurch camp-site. Simply turn left to return to the car-park.

Historical Notes

The River Wye has its source on the foothills of Plynlimmon, deep in Central Wales. This, too, is the birthplace of that other great Gloucestershire river – the Severn. These rivers take very different courses to their confluence at Chepstow, and with the Wye passing through essentially rural areas with little industrial or commercial development, it is widely held to be one of Britain's most beautiful rivers. Below Ross, the Wye Valley supports a staggering 65 species of native trees and shrubs, whilst the alkaline limestone and the acidic sandstone of the region support a diverse range of flora. The scenery in the area is held to be some of the finest in Europe. During the 18th and 19th centuries, Severn trows worked the Wye as far as Brockweir, 8 miles upstream of Chepstow. At Brockweir, all cargoes had to be offloaded onto smaller barges to work the river as far as Ross and Hereford. The Wye carried more than commercial freight. 1782 saw the publication of Gilpin's *Observations on the River Wye and Several Points in South Wales.* This was essentially an early guide book to the region, giving publicity to a two-day excursion from Ross-on-Wye to Chepstow. By 1827, eight covered rowboats a day were leaving Ross for the stylish cruise downstream, providing facilities for visitors to sit and eat, as well as sketch, draw and write.

The Wye is also a noted salmon water, due primarily to its cleanliness and continual flushing and oxygenation by its tributary streams. Queen Elizabeth I, for example, sold some land around Monmouth but deliberately 'retained the tithes of salmon and other fish to be taken in the waters and rivers within the parish of Monmouth'. In 1923, a salmon weighing 59½ pounds and measuring 52½ inches was rod-caught in the Wye, whilst a few years earlier a dead specimen weighing 80 pounds and measuring 59½ inches was washed up.

The Ross and Monmouth Railway, whose trackbed the ramble follows alongside the rive Wye to Symonds Yat, was authorised in 1865. Progress was slow, however, and this single line whose main custom came from tourists to the area, did not actually open until 4th August 1873. Between Ross and Monmouth, there were stations at Kerne Bridge, Lydbrook and Symonds Yat. Run by the Great Western Railway, a line in such a sparsely populated region as the Wye Valley was never going to be much of a money-spinner. There were tourists aplenty, but the tourist season was very short-lived. An enquiry a short while before the line was closed revealed an annual loss of £10,000 per annum – this compared with the annual loss of just £1,500 on the parallel bus service. The conclusion was all too obvious, and passenger services were withdrawn on 5th January 1959.

Symonds Yat Rock is a 500 ft bluff situated high above the river Wye as it encircles Huntsham Hill. From the viewpoint, it actually looks as if there are two rivers down below in the valley, with the missing link having disappeared behind Huntsham Hill. The views are magnificent, and the topograph at the site offers a far better description of the landmarks than a mere guide-book writer ever could! South-east of the viewpoint lie Coldwell Rocks, on which any number of pairs of binoculars have been focussed since 1982. During that year, after a 30 year absence, peregrine falcons returned to nest on the rock ledges. For many years, the peregrine falcon had been threatened by DDT creeping into the food chain through its widespread use on arable farms. With the banning of DDT, the peregrine falcons have become regular breeders at Coldwell Rocks, with several young being reared each year.

The name 'yat' is actually Old English for 'gate'. There was a pass through the Iron Age fortifications near the summit of the rock, and this in all probability is where the name 'yat' originated. The fortifications, shown clearly on local 1:25,000 OS sheets, consist of a series of banks and ditches some 2,000 years old. The cliff-to-cliff ramparts formed a promontory fort, enclosing a site of some 10 acres centred on the present day car-park.

Glasshouse, May Hill and Newent Woods

Introduction: May Hill is, I suspect, Gloucestershire's best known yet least visited landmark. Its 971 ft summit, decked out with a clump of pine trees, is familiar to the millions of motorists who travel up and down the M5 motorway between Bristol and Worcester each year. Equally, many walkers following the Cotswold Way will have pointed out the round mass of old sandstone with its crown of trees that marks the real boundary of the English plain. Beyond rise the foothills of the Welsh mountains. Few travellers, however, venture towards the Herefordshire border to seek out this lonely and isolated spot. The effort is well worthwhile for, in addition to the quite magnificent views over many neighbouring counties, the walk brings the opportunity to stroll through the well known Newent Woods. As a seasonal excursion, springtime is especially rewarding as the woods burst into colour with wild daffodils and bluebells.

Distance: A 4 mile circuit, with a steady climb of over 550 ft from Clifford's Mesne to the summit of May Hill. A good proportion of the route lies along quiet country lanes, rather than public footpaths. Allow 2½ to 3 hours.

Refreshments: The Glasshouse Inn is conveniently located at the end of the walk. At Clifford's Mesne, just before the climb onto May Hill, the walk passes the Yew Tree Inn.

How to get there: Glasshouse lies one mile north of Huntley and Dursley Cross, midway between Gloucester and Ross-on-Wye on the A40. Follow the signposts to the Glasshouse, where there is room for parking on the green opposite the Glasshouse Inn. (GR 709204)

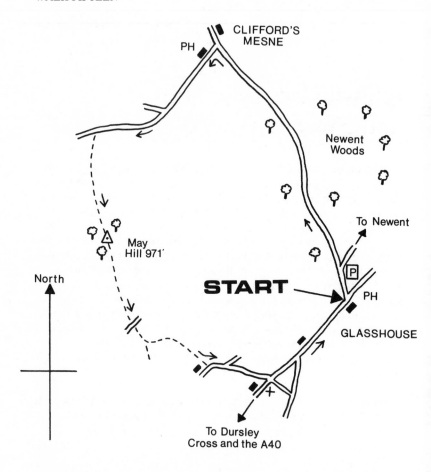

The Walk: From the Glasshouse Inn, follow the minor road through Newent Woods to Clifford's Mesne. There are public footpaths through the trees that run almost parallel to this quiet country road, but I found these to be heavily overgrown and the route virtually impossible to describe.

In Clifford's Mesne, take the first turning on the left signposted to the Yew Tree Inn. This cul-de-sac lane climbs steadily onto the National Trust's May Hill Common. 400 yards on from the cattle grid that gives you access to the common, the lane forks. Bear left and continue for ½ mile until you come to a gateway on the left-hand side. Turn left, and head uphill along the wide grassy ride that climbs towards May Hill itself. The views almost defy description – simply enjoy them as some form of compensation for the stiff leg muscles and overworked lungs that you might be experiencing!

Towards the top of the climb, cross an obvious stile alongside a National Trust sign and continue across a rough pasture to reach the pine clump, planted to commemorate the Golden Jubilee of Queen Victoria, that adorns the top of May Hill. This viewpoint offers magnificent views of the Severn Vale, the Cotswolds and the Brecon Beacons.

Suitably rested, continue along the same path as it follows a well-defined course down the southern slopes of the hillside to a handgate, with the Severn Vale opening up in front of you. The enclosed path continues downhill to a crossroads. Continue straight ahead, bear left at a distinct fork and carry on until you reach a quiet country lane. Turn left, and head downhill to a road junction, ignoring the one no-through-road you pass en route. At the junction, turn left to return to Glasshouse, all the while enjoying the views northwards of the Malvern Hills. You will soon be back at the Glasshouse Inn where the walk began.

Historical Notes

Glasshouse: The sign outside the Glasshouse Inn, depicting glass workers toiling at their labours, gives a distinct clue as to the origins of this settlement. In the early years of the 17th century, as the demand for glass in Britain was growing, glassmakers from Lorraine in France brought their skills across the Channel. A small works was established in this corner of Gloucestershire, using wood from the nearby Newent Woods to produce charcoal. This was then used as a fuel source in the manufacturing process. As the 17th century drew to a close, the local timber supplies proved inadequate as the demand for glass soared. The glassmakers moved off to the Staffordshire coalfield, leaving only a place-name as evidence of their labours. The field where the works was located lies on the right-hand side as you walk along the Clifford's Mesne road. Look carefully just as you cross a stream about 100 yards from the Glasshouse Inn.

May Hill is what the geologist would describe as a 'dome' of old rock, rock that is in fact similar to the sandstones that form the nearby Malvern Hills. The hilltop and adjoining May Hill Common are both National Trust properties, and the Trust's handbook quite accurately describes the area as 'wild and romantic'. The views from May Hill are some of the finest views to be found anywhere in Gloucestershire. To the north lie the Malvern Hills, rising to 1,394 ft at the Worcester Beacon. To the south lies the Forest of Dean, whose wooded slopes tumble down towards the Severn Estuary. The vast horseshoe-bend that the river's waters have carved around Arlingham is clearly visible. The eastern skyline is dominated by the Cotswold Edge, whilst to the west rise the Black Mountains and the Brecon Beacons, a very real reminder that this is border country. Ysgyryd Fawr (1,595 ft) and the Sugar Loaf (1,955 ft), just north of Abergavenny, are especially prominent peaks. The clump of trees that make May Hill such an instantly recognisable landmark were planted in 1887 to mark Queen Victoria's Golden Jubilee.